# Aryani East and West

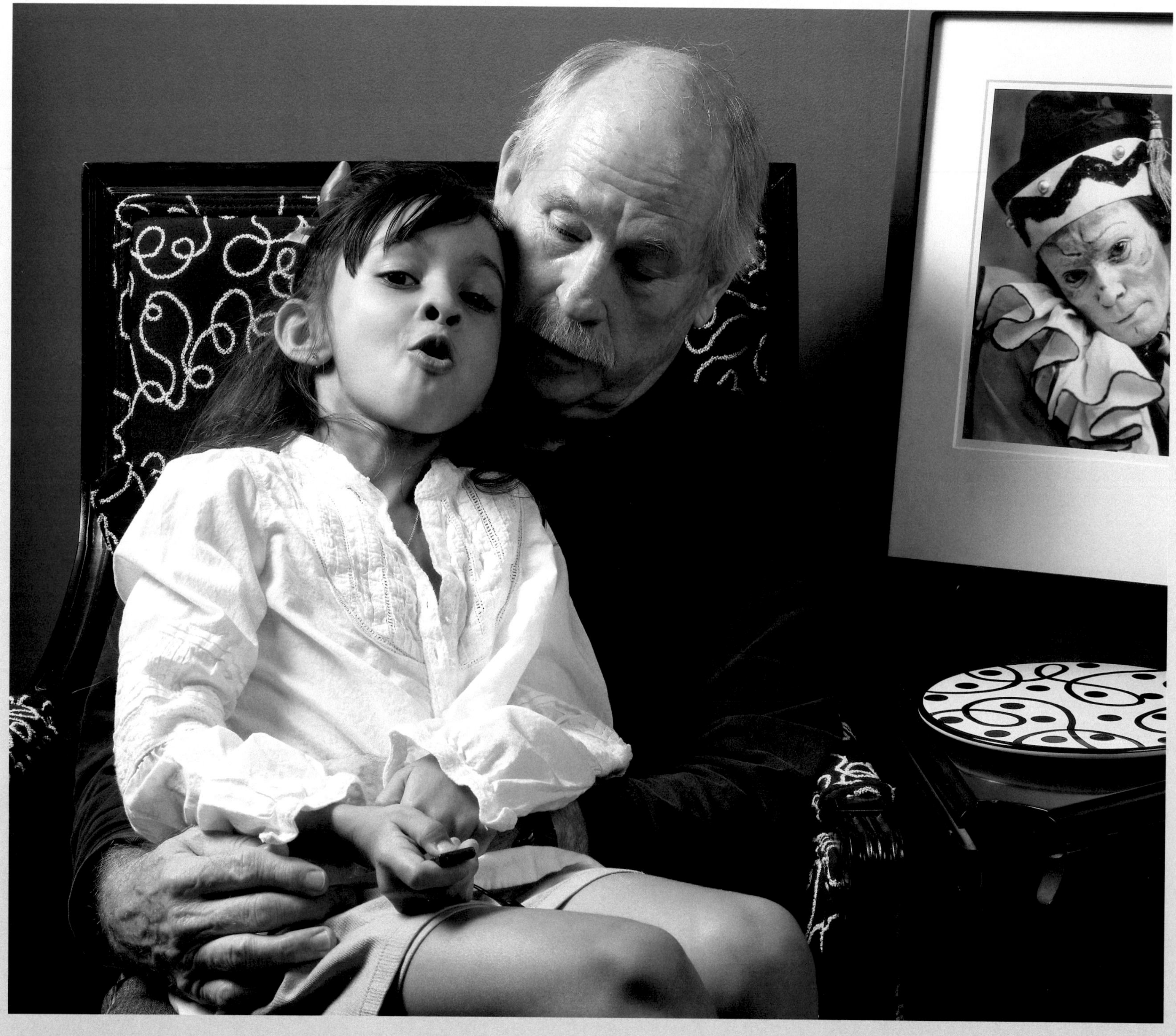

# Aryani
# East and West

A Photographic Collaboration between

Aryani Odie and Martin Miller

The Chelsea Press

*Aryani East and West*
by Martin Miller



First Edition, First Printing

Library of Congress Control Number: 2024913254
ISBN 978-0-9862127-3-4

The Chelsea Press
Baltimore, Maryland

Printed in the United States of America

ALSO BY MARTIN MILLER:

*Intimations: Intuitions beyond Subject*, The Chelsea Press, 2022

*Triumph and Tragedy: The Evolution and Legacy of 20th Century War Machines*, The Chelsea Press, 2021

*Weapons of Mass Destruction: Specters of the Nuclear Age*, Schiffer Publishing, Ltd., 2017.

*The Neutron's Long Shadow: Legacies of Nuclear Explosives Production in the Manhattan Project*, Schiffer Publishing, Ltd., 2017.

FOR FURTHER INFORMATION PLEASE VISIT

www.Martin-Miller.us
www.WorldWarWorks.com
www.TheChelseaPress.com
www.Aryani.us

for

Mama, Nana, Deshi,
Sleepy Mama, David,
and Grandma Gail

In a Wonderland they lie,
Dreaming as the days go by,
Dreaming as the summers die:
Ever drifting down the stream—
Lingering in the golden gleam—
Life, what is it but a dream?

—Lewis Carroll,
Through the Looking Glass (1871)

# About the Book

With a father reared in the western tradition and a mother from the Hindu culture, Aryani has a foot in both worlds. Trained in the demanding art of classical Bharatanatyam Indian dance, she has performed solos from age five. At age nine she played the lead role of Belle in her school's production of Beauty and the Beast. Besides dancing, singing, and acting, she is also an accomplished pianist. For some seven years photographer Martin Miller, her grandfather, conducted formal photoshoots in her home and in his home, adding modeling to her long list of talents. He also photographed her during her Indian dance performances. Herein is the wonderful result of a unique collaboration between a photographer and his young and gifted model, between a grandfather and his granddaughter.

This book documents Aryani's transformation from early childhood onto the doorstep of womanhood; it only hints at the depths of this exceptional human being. She revels in being a "girly girl" and finds singular expression of her personality in the dress of both western and Hindu cultures. Her extraordinary talent for the Bharatanatyam Indian dance provides further expressive outlet through gesture and movement, both nuanced and athletic. The book celebrates an extraordinary confluence of eastern and western cultures, but, more than anything else, it is a timeless statement of love and mutual respect between very different generations.

Note: Videos of Aryani's dance perfornances, including The Jungle Book, may be viewed at www.Aryani.us.

# Preface

During my 50+ years as a photographer, landscape and documentary photography have been my oeurve—until now. This project actually began in 2012 when Aryani was not yet three years old, and I had the idea to incorporate photographs of deep-space nebulae from the Hubble telescope into my landscape photographs to produce a surreal, other-worldly effect. As the idea evolved in my head, I thought that the effect might be enhanced if only children could see these astonishing displays and adults would be insensitive to their presence. Right under my nose was my cute little granddaughter, Aryani. The first image planned was to be from my living room where Aryani would gaze out the front window in wonder at the nebula filled sky, and my wife, her Grandma Gail, would be reading the newspaper—oblivious to the celestial display just outside the window. However, when the studio lights were set up, with their heavy black wires crisscrossing the floor, connecting scary, flashing electrical boxes to tall stands where the strobe lights hung, festooned with large umbrella reflectors, Aryani was having none of it. Nothing I said could change her mind.

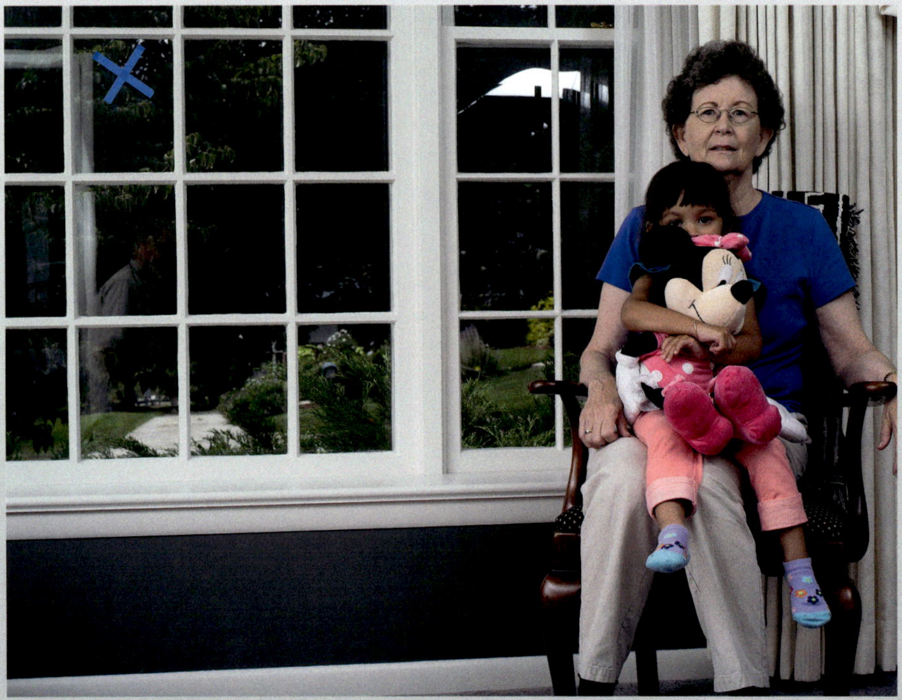

2012/06/19, 12:44:55 pm

Clearly, this was a job for Grandma Gail. It turned out to be no pushover for her, either. After showing little fear herself of these alien contrivances nearly filling our small living room, Grandma Gail soothed and coaxed until Aryani agreed to sit on her lap at a safe distance and peer at the threat through the ears of her outsized Minnie Mouse from the comforting confines of grandma's arms. It was now ok for me, the bringer of these dark presences, to rejoin the family group.

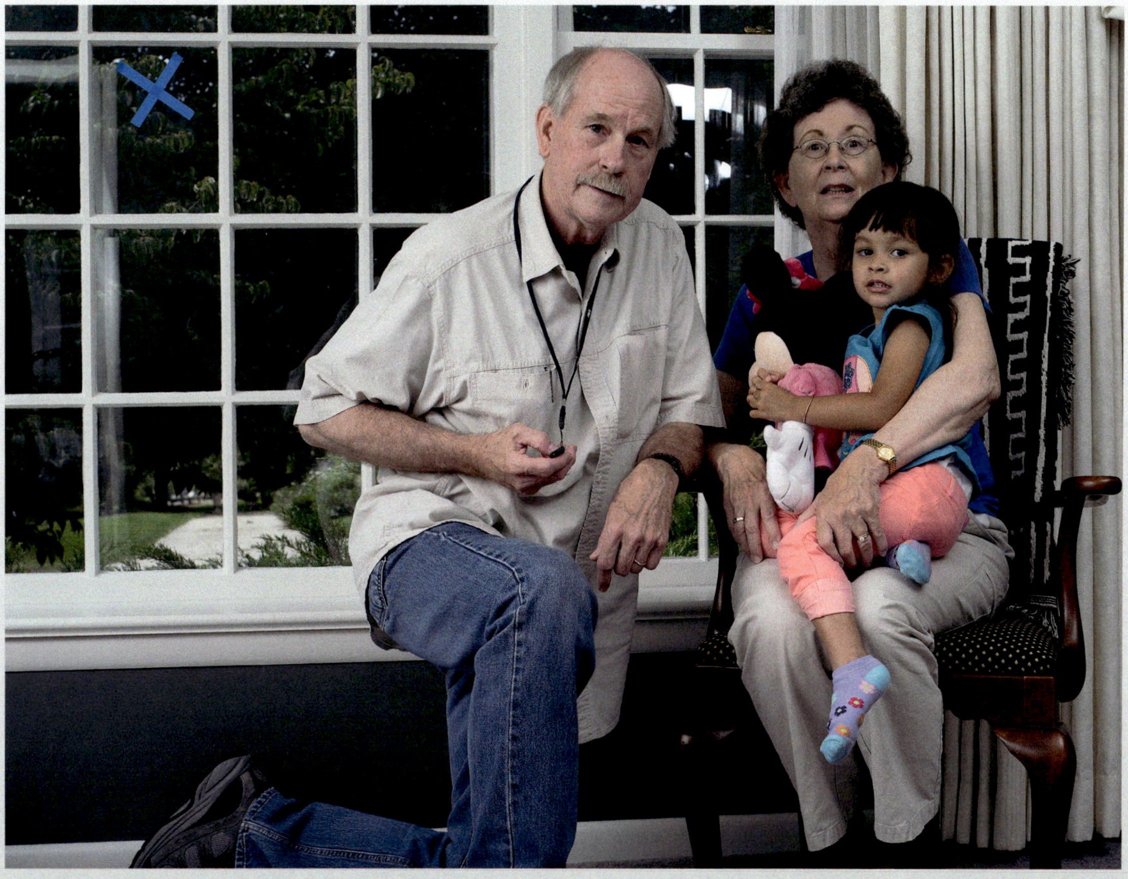

2012/06/19, 12:47:03 pm

The only trick I had up my sleeve at this point was actually around my neck—the wireless shutter release for the camera. Like everyone else, Aryani became fascinated with the action-at-a-distance power of bending the powerful light flashes to her will. We could also run to the camera after every shot and see the wondrous images she had just made. Still, with some lingering apprehension, she sat next to me at the window and

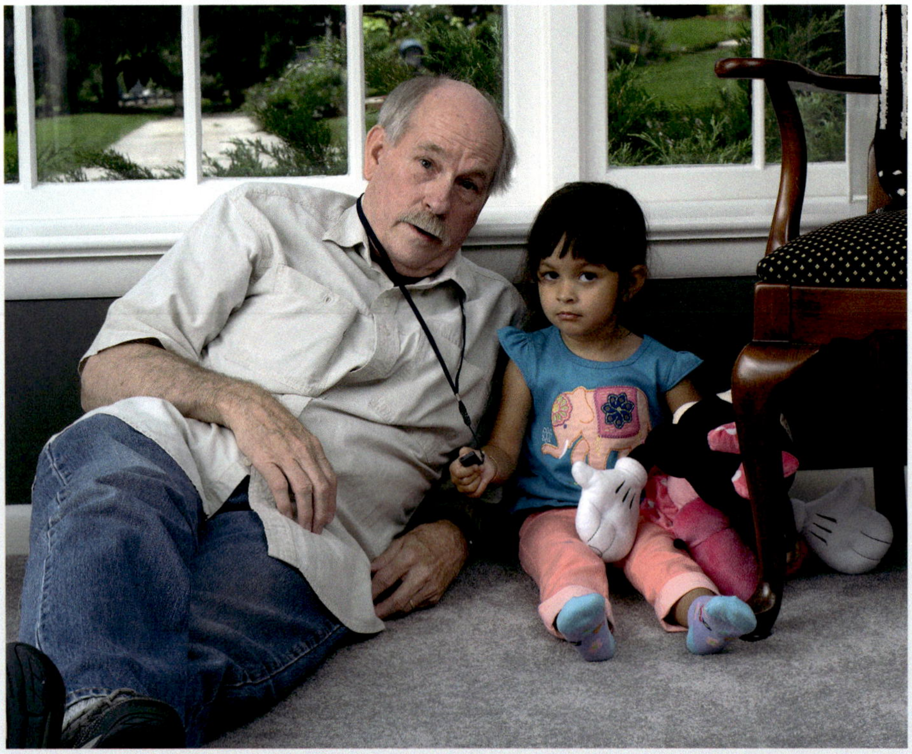

2012/06/19, 1:05:57 pm

worked the magic button around my neck. Grandma Gail could at last take her leave. Growing bolder by degrees, she at last stood apart from me, entrusting Minnie Mouse

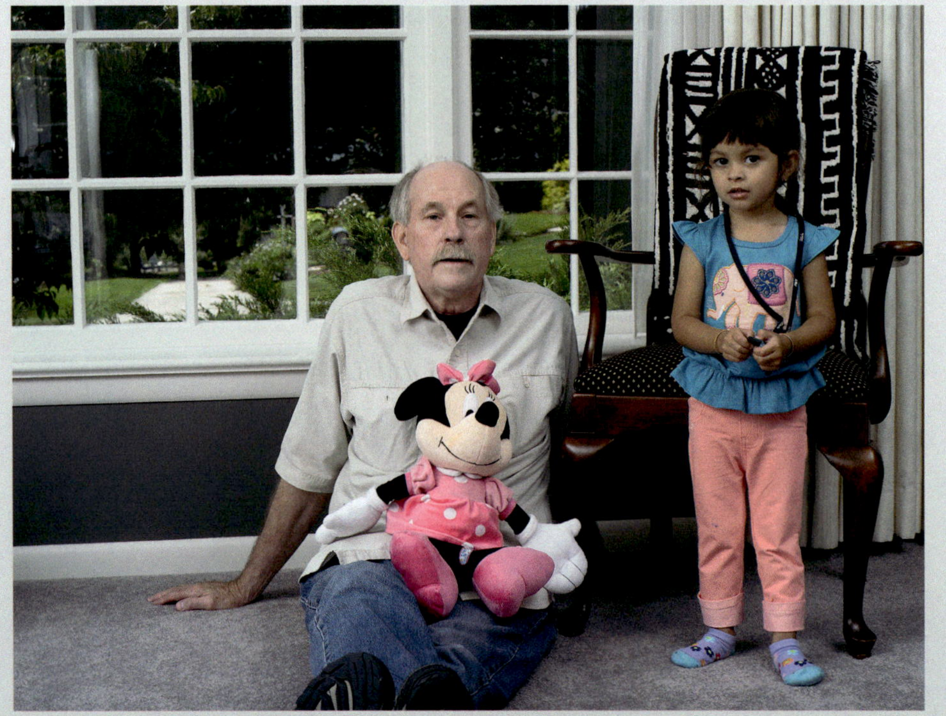

2012/06/19, 1:10:49 pm

to my lap, and warmed to her newfound role as mistress of the frightful beast. Now I could get on with my planned image making. Aryani was no longer afraid and fully invested in my project, though she had little comprehension of what final image I was aiming for. However, she gamely posed again and again until I was satisfied that I had what I needed. Each final image consisted of a mosaic of some dozen individual overlapping photographs stitched together into a high resolution whole with specialized software. Here

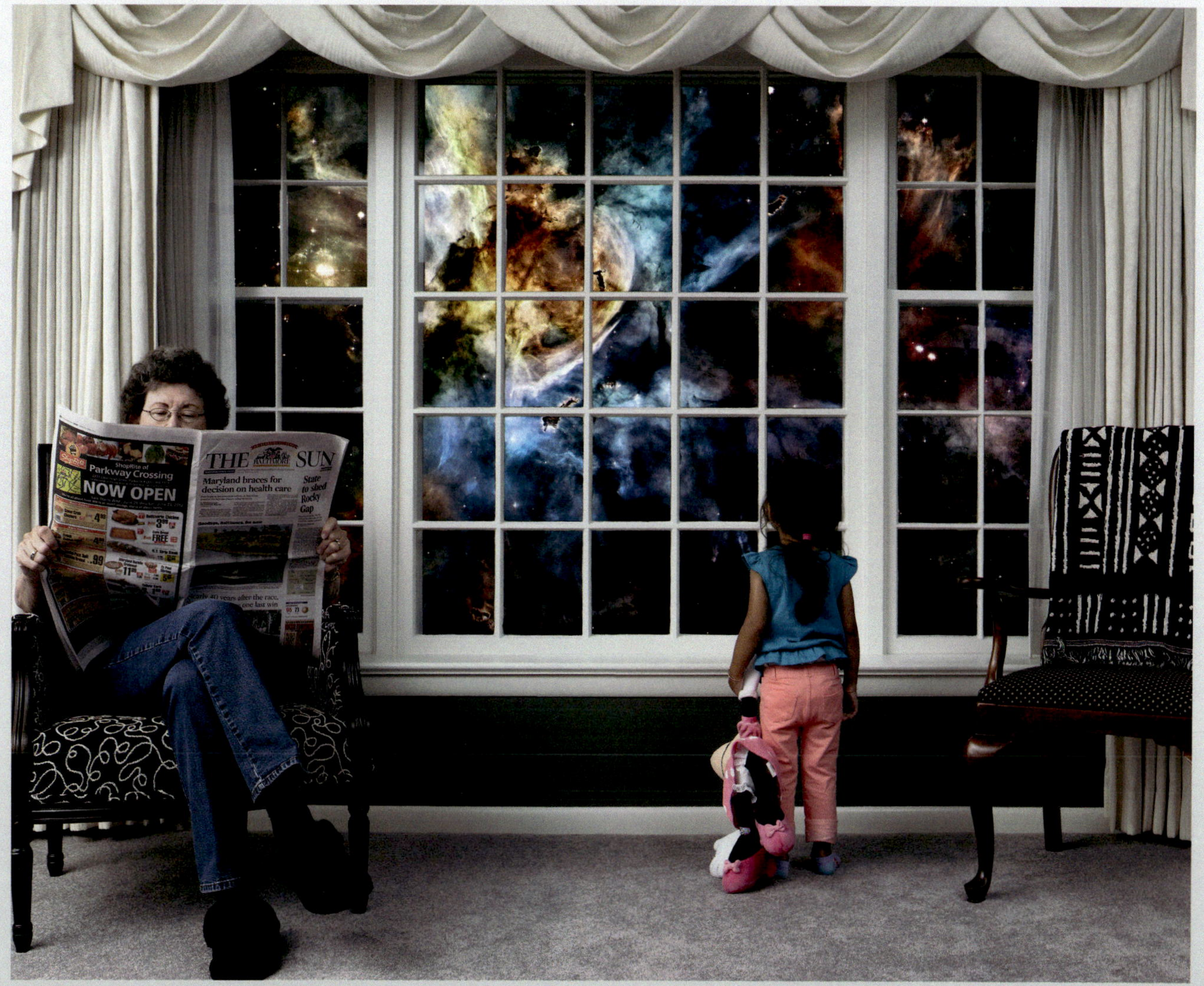

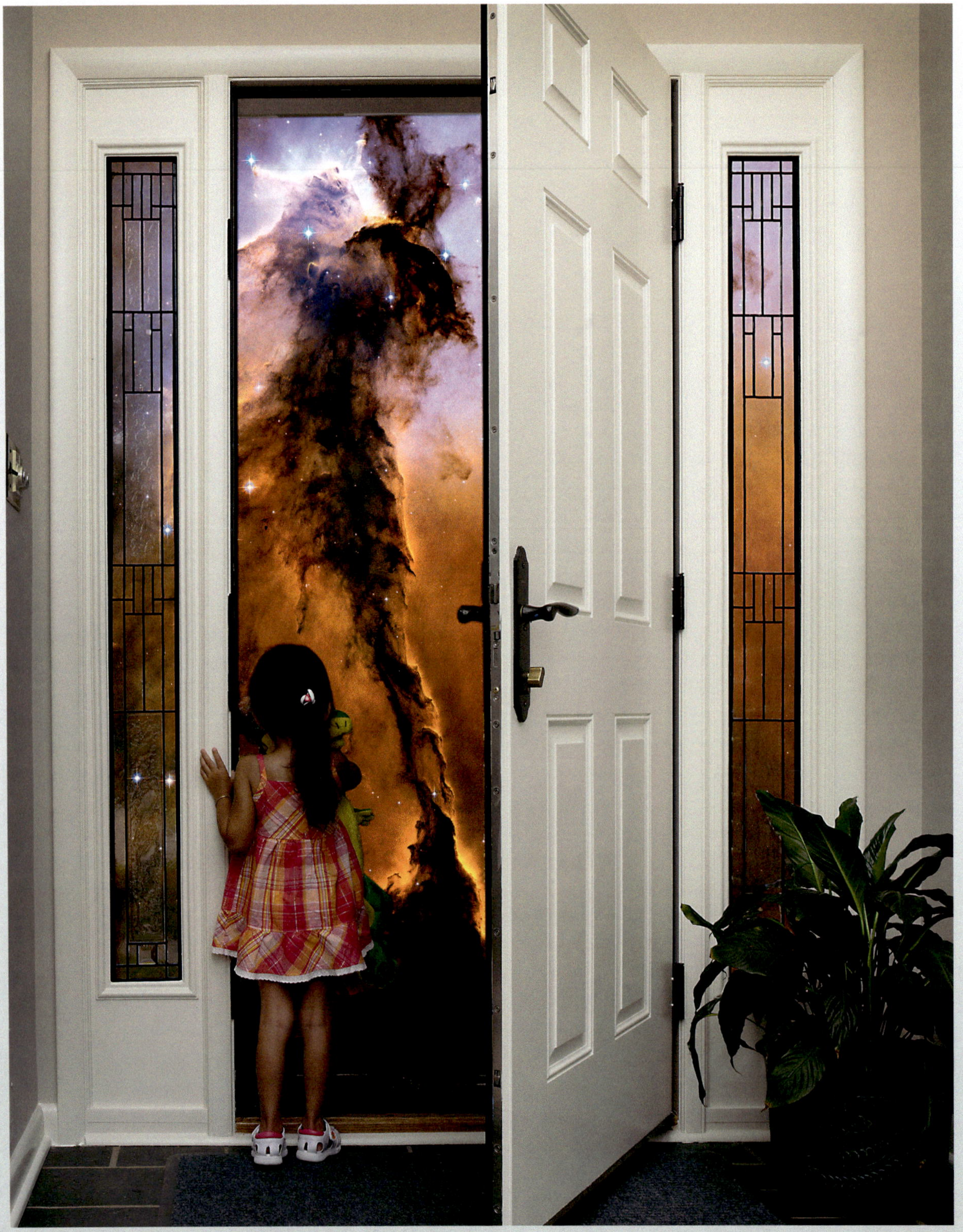

are the results of this and another day's photoshoot (and many hours of computer work afterward). The Hubble project itself did not go much further than this, but the seed for working with Aryani as a model had been planted. Three more years would pass before a chance rediscovery of Lewis Carroll's photographs of Alice Liddell, the inspiration for his Alice's Adventures in Wonderland, would launch us on the project presented in this book.

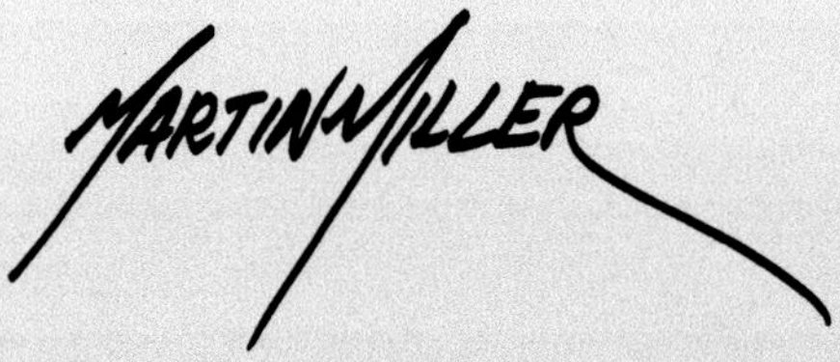

# About the Photographs

I am quintessentially a black and white photographer. I have had forays into the world of color—the Hubble images on the previous pages would lose much of their other-worldly impact in black and white—and I admire the fine color photography of others. But my experience is that color photographs most often end up being about color itself. For me fine black and white photographs best express and distill the essence of the subject through tone, form, and texture. This is why Lewis Carroll's photographs spoke so persuasively to me as inspiration for the Aryani project. A counter argument could easily be made, was made by Aryani herself, that much of the splendor of the Hindu culture is to be found in color—the extravagant dance costumes, the Holi festival of colors, etc. As all of the images shown here were originally captured in color, I had a choice. In the end I compromised and decided to present the images involving Hindu costumes in color and the rest of the photographs in black and white. In converting to black and white, it is literally true that something is lost, but in the metaphysical dimension I maintain that something also is gained. In this book one image is shown both in black and white and color versions to give the viewer a direct comparison of the tradeoffs. The feeling of each is very different—one more abstract and cerebrally aesthetic, the other luxurient and rife with emotion. I hope that the viewer will find pleasure in them both.

A conspicuous eccentricity of the following gallery of images is the date/time stamp associated with each image. Few people will care to know the exact moment of exposure down to the fraction of a second, but photography is all about capturing the moment, and digital cameras make it possible to know exactly which moment was actually captured. Coupled with my spare captions, the date/time stamp will enable the reader to follow the chronology of Aryani's journey through childhood.

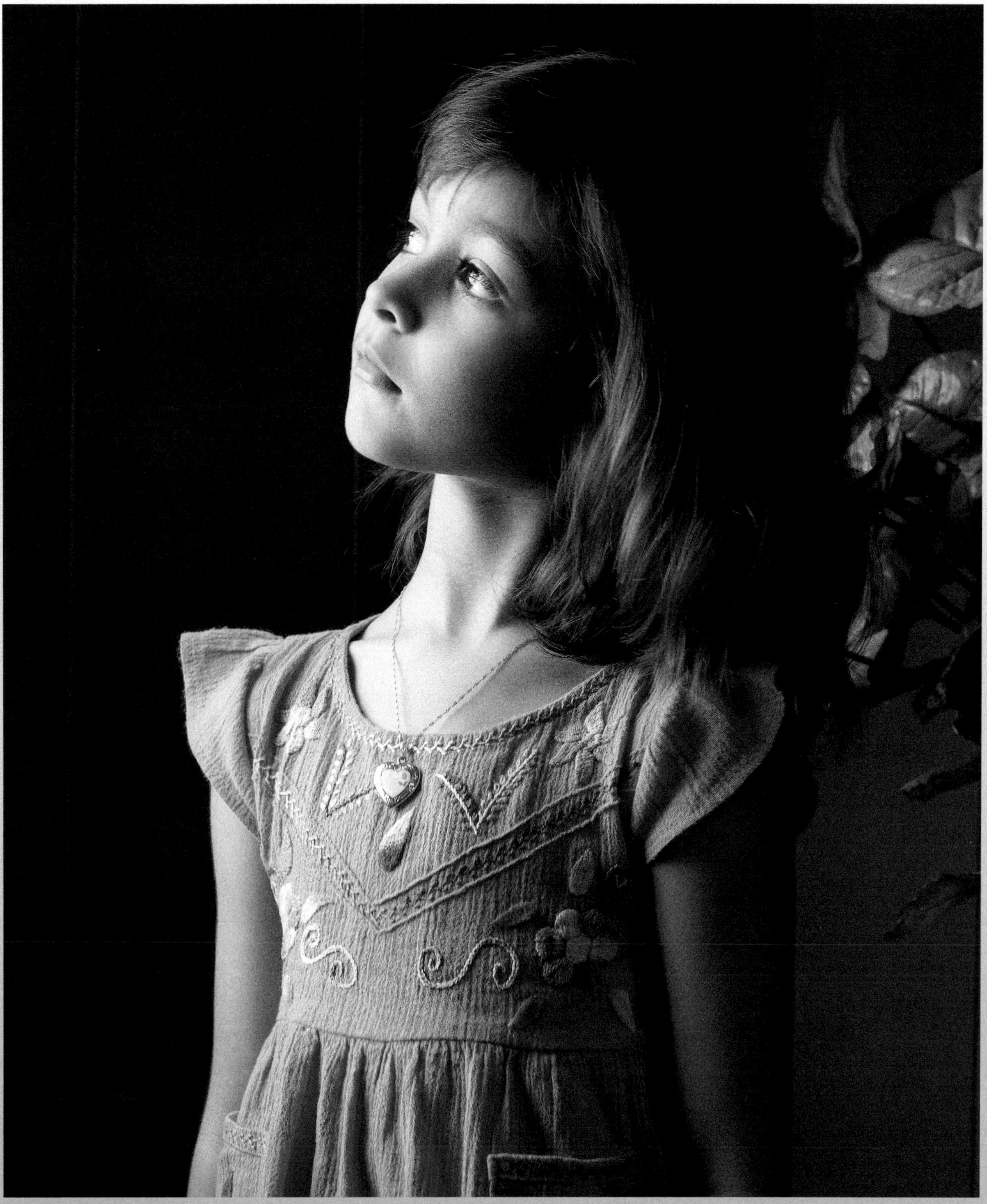

Aryani not long after her sixth birthday

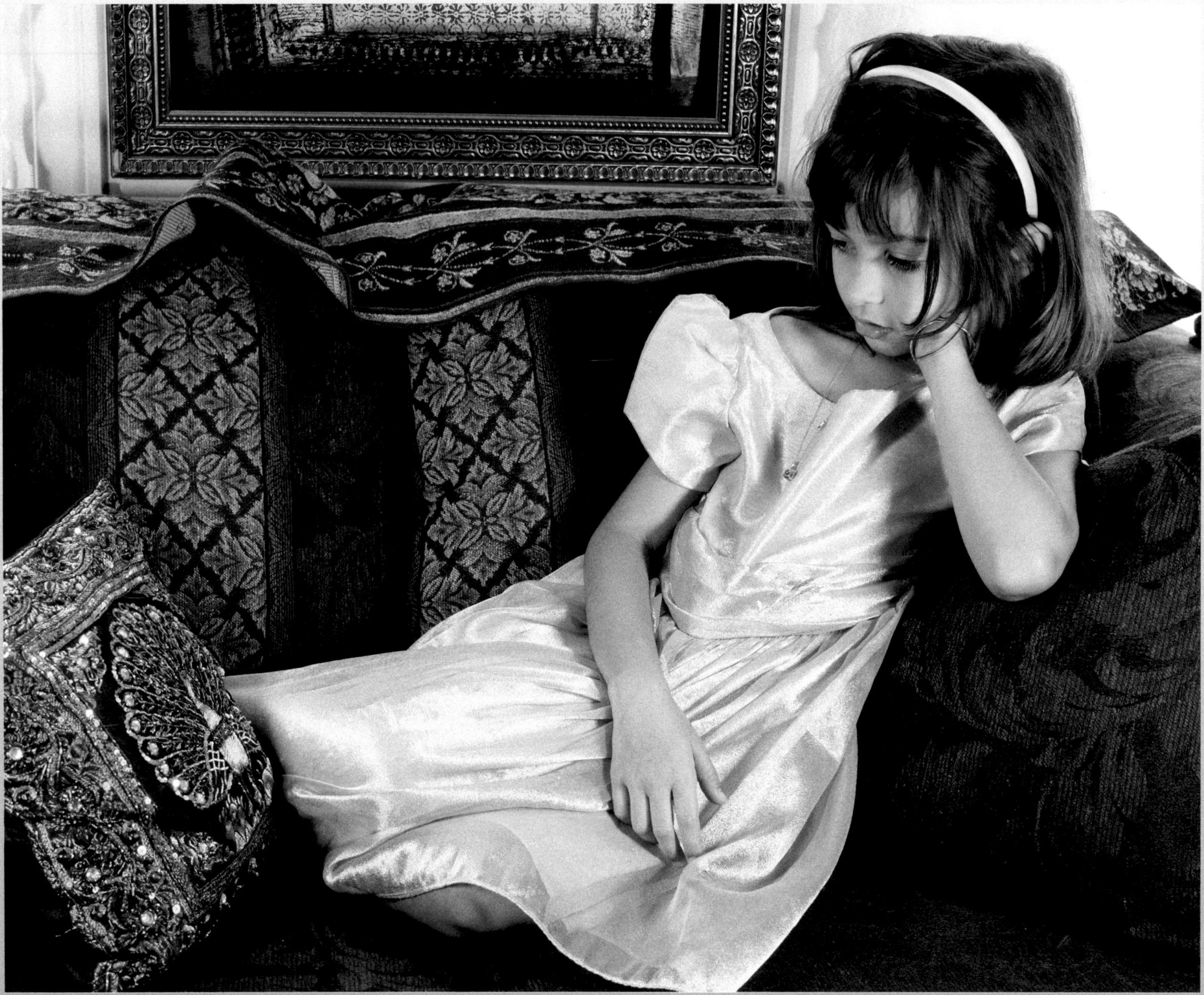

A pensive Aryani at six years old.

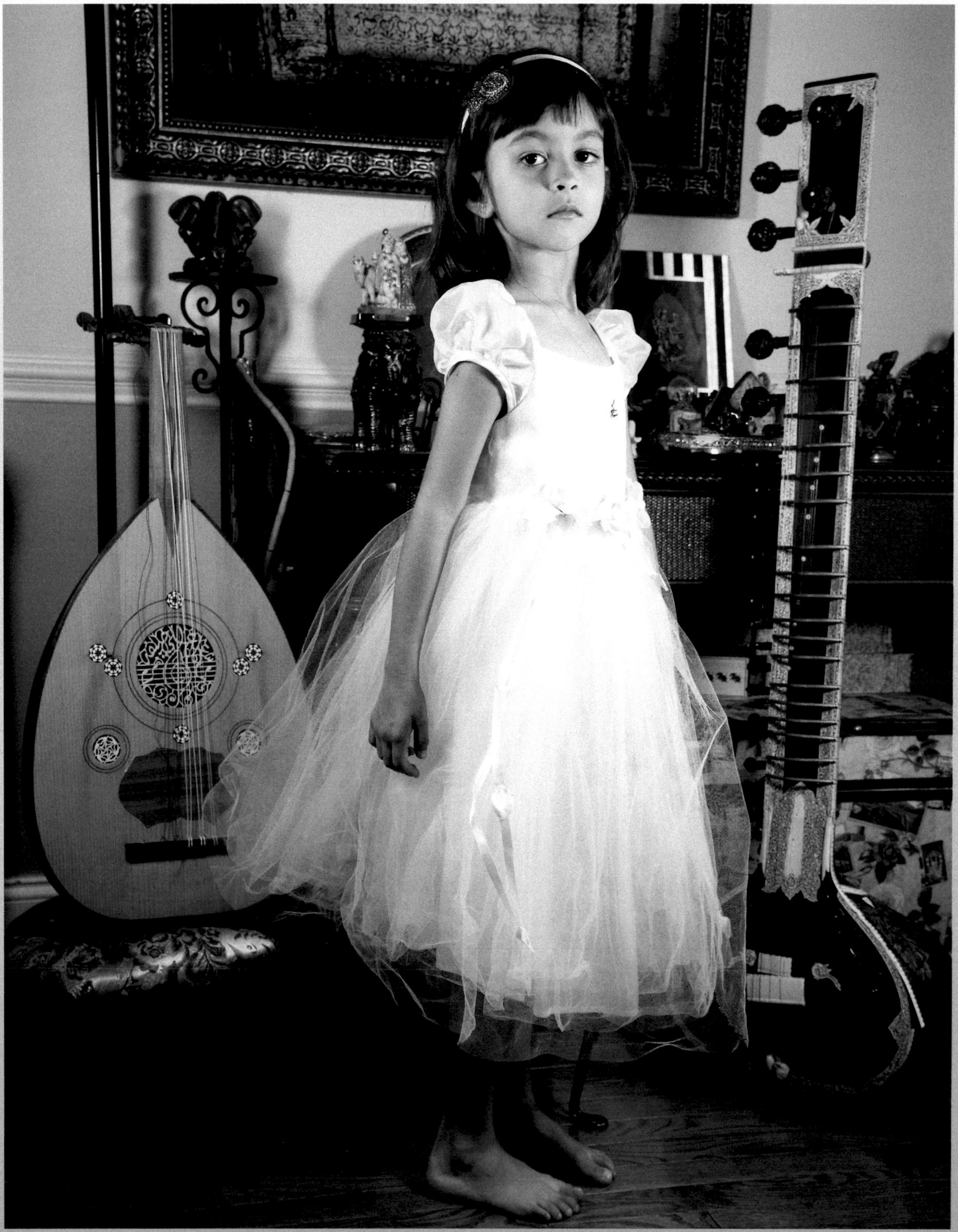

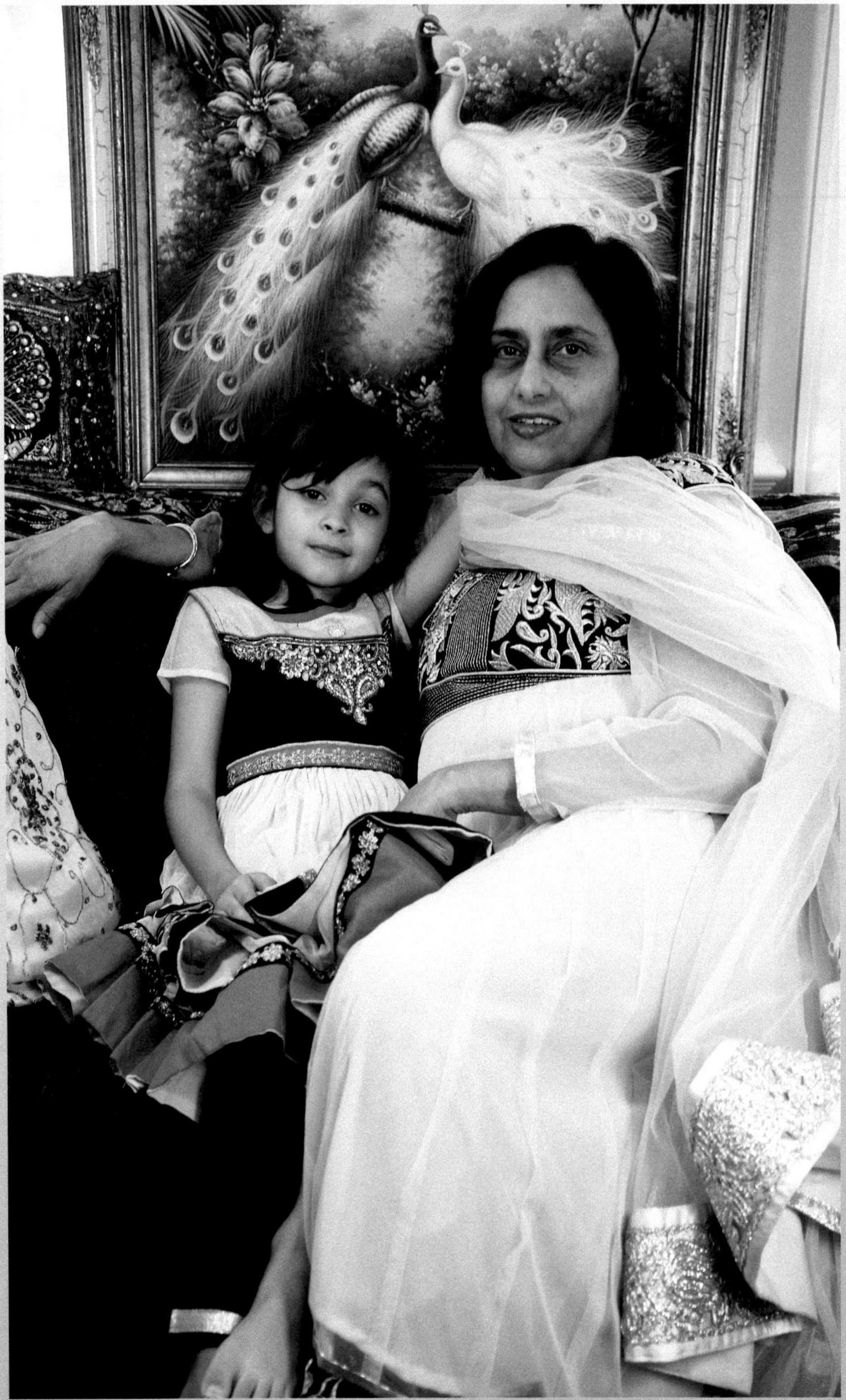

Aryani and Mama portrayed in black and white and in color under ideal lighting conditions. I can understand

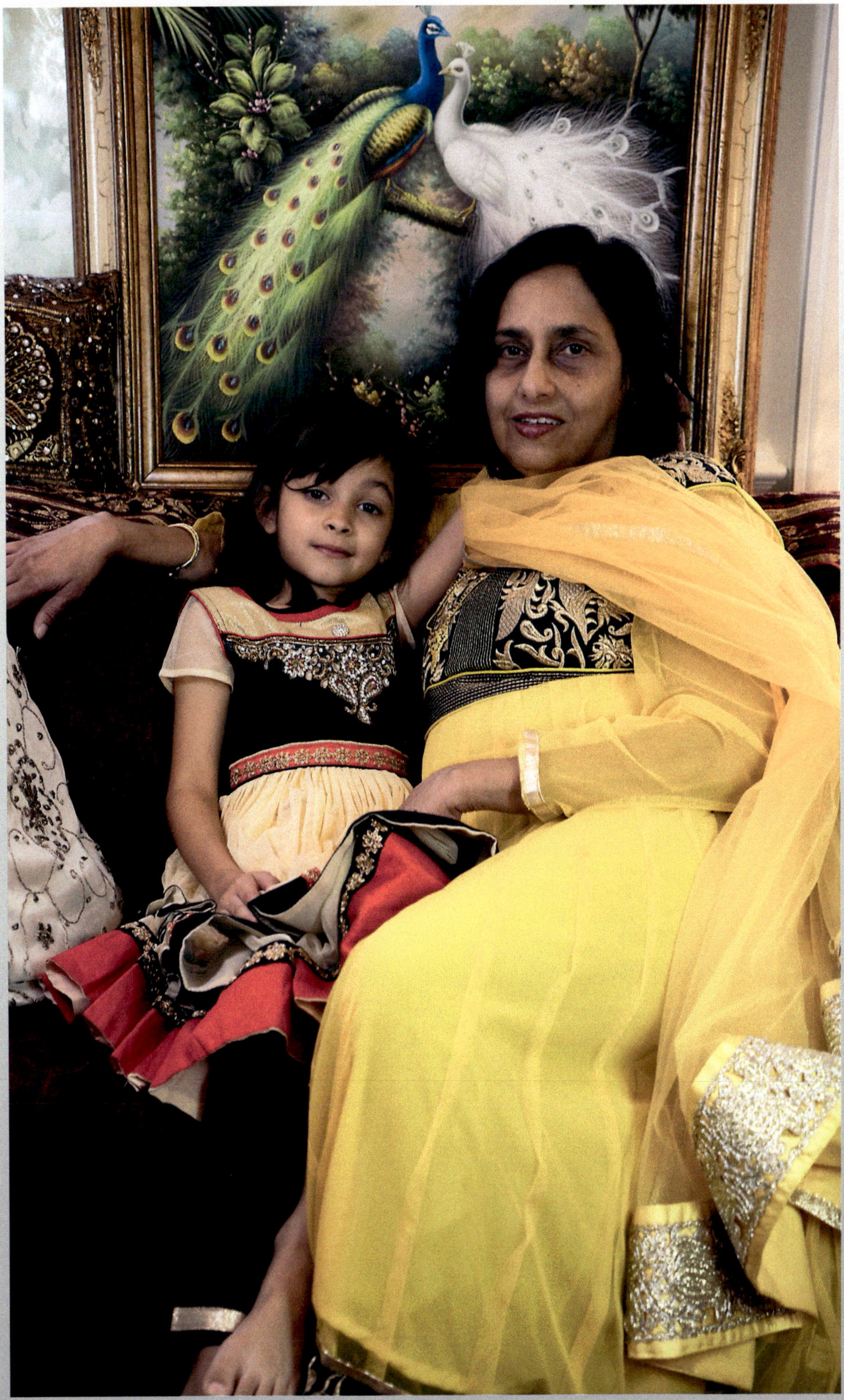

why some may prefer the color version, but for me the B&W version is unmatched for purity and sublimity.

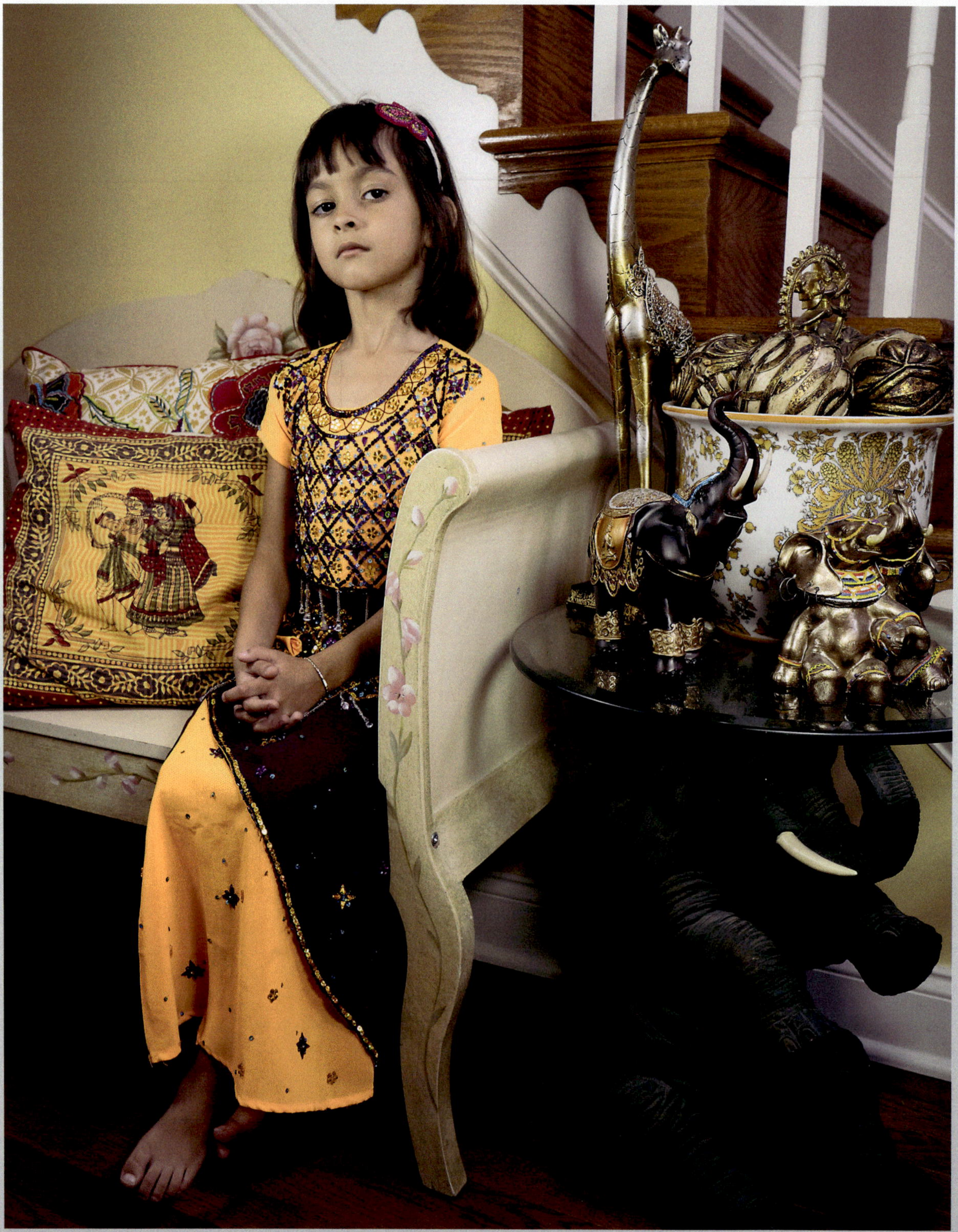

The elephant table

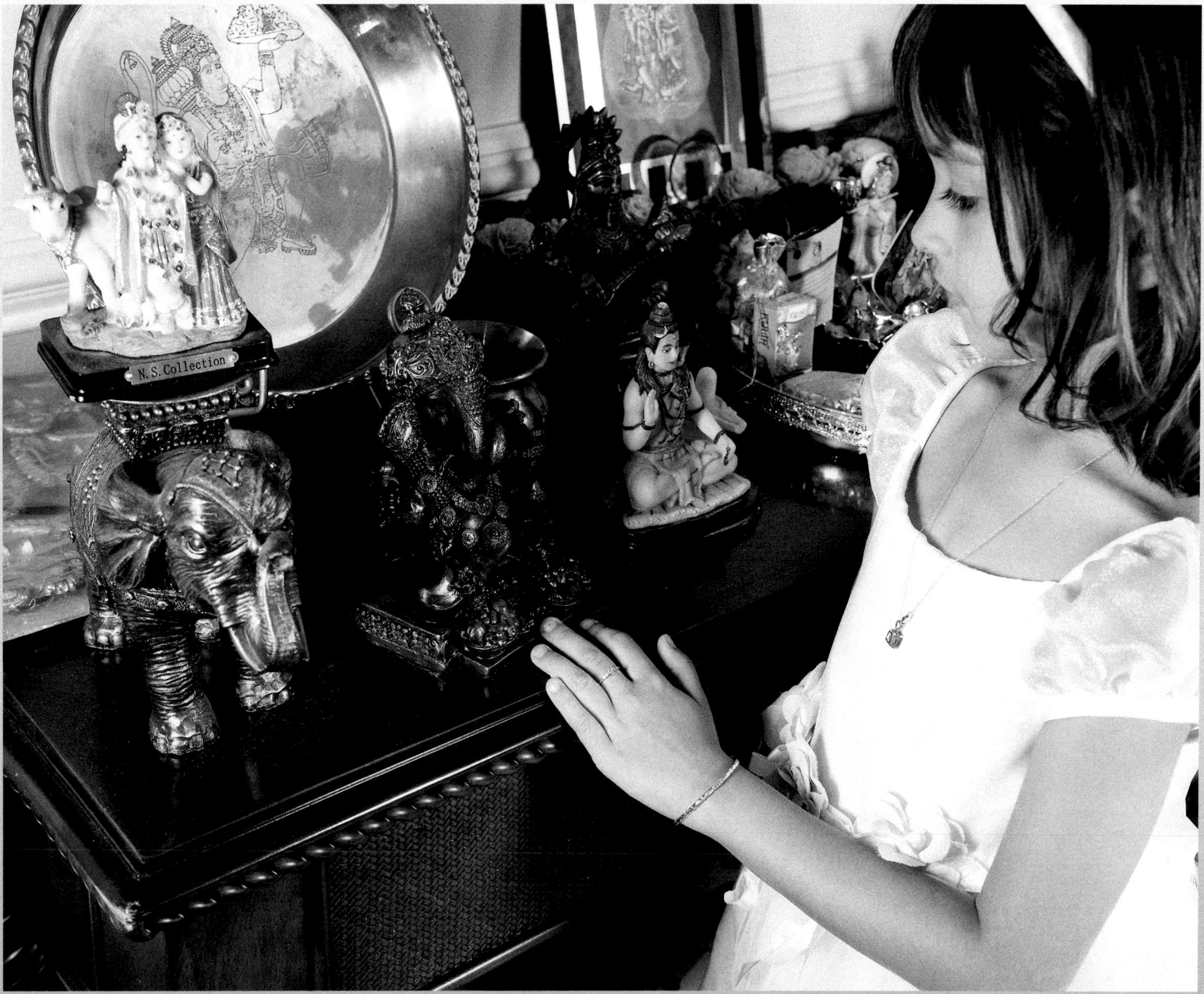


The ikon table

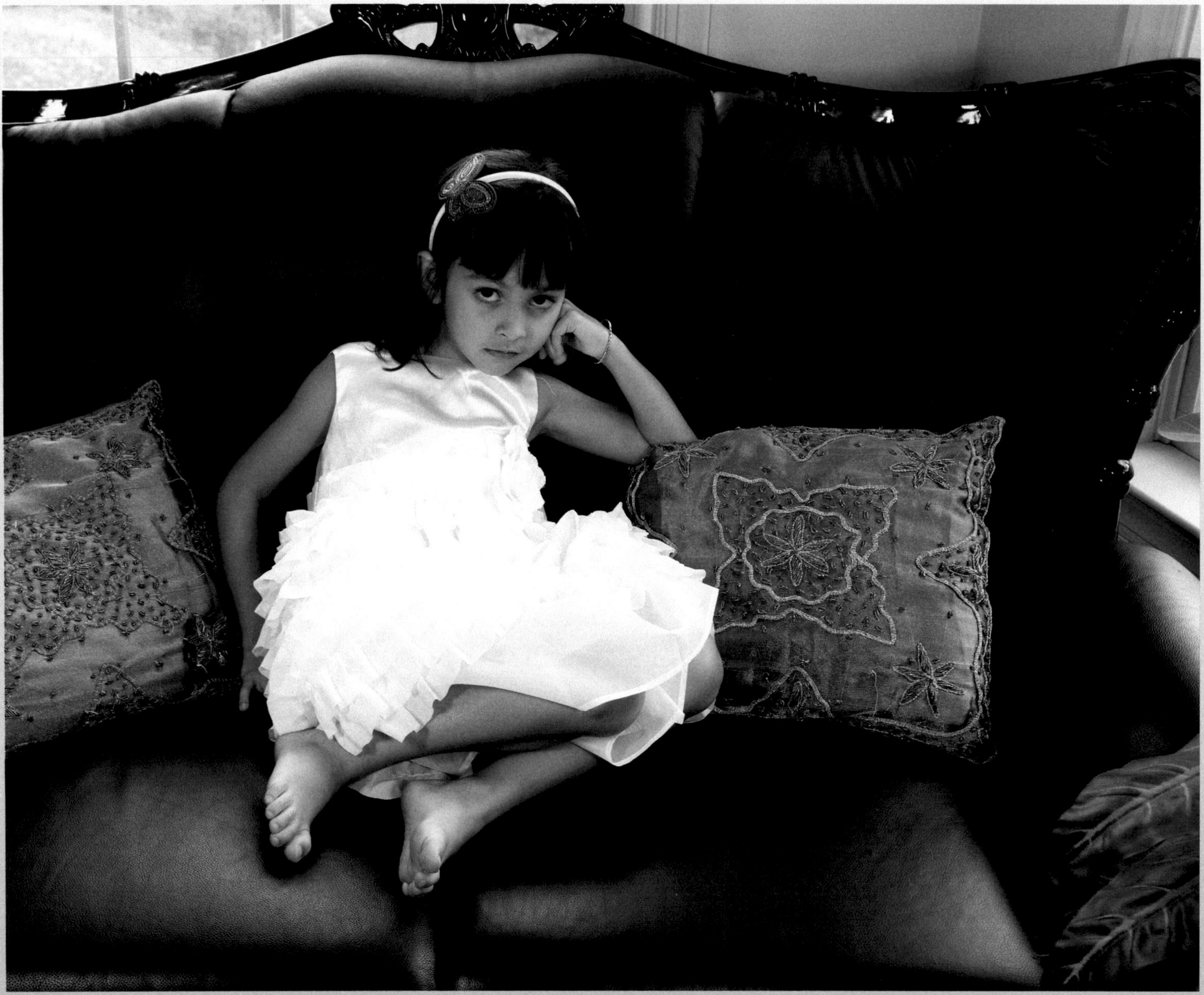

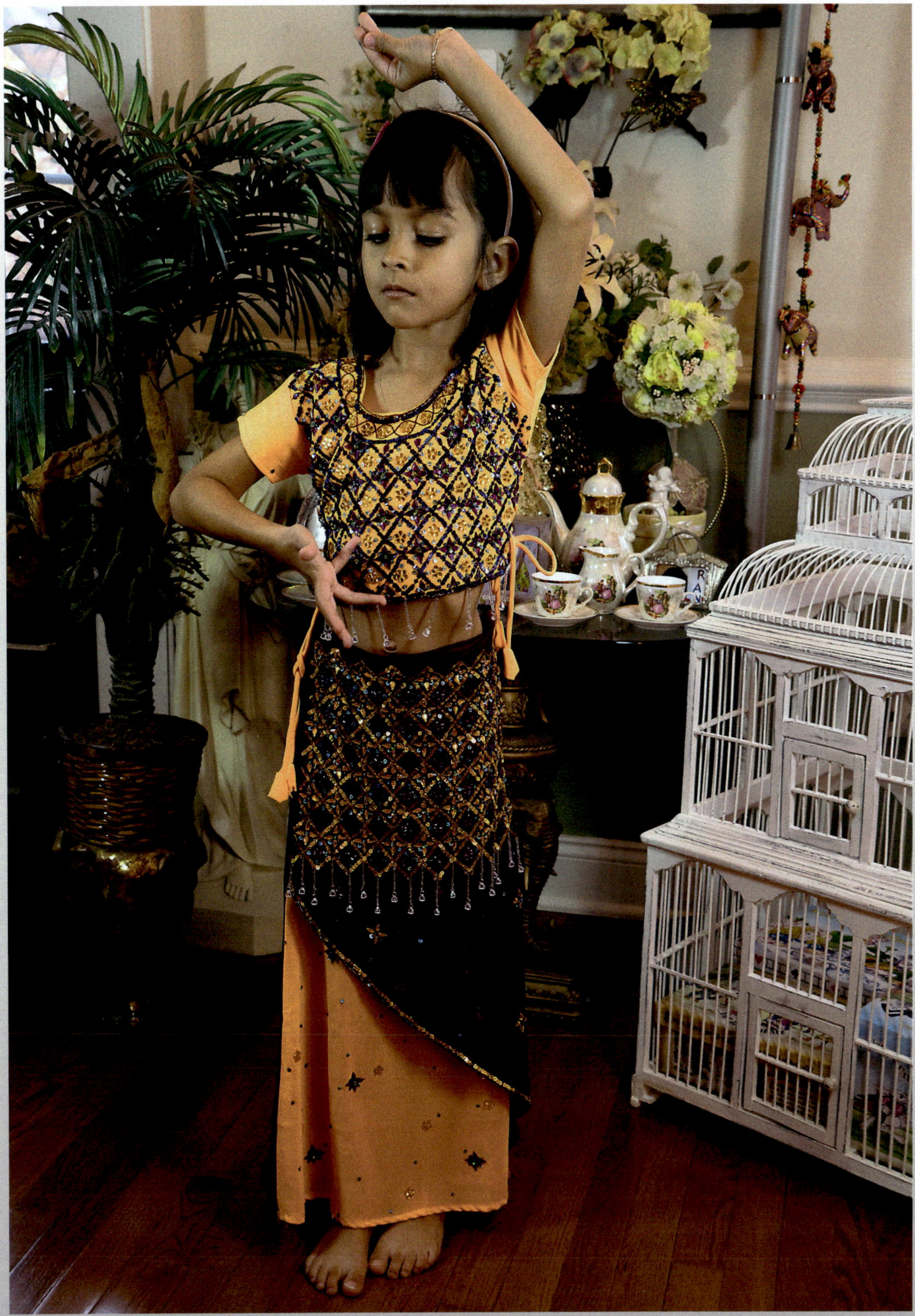

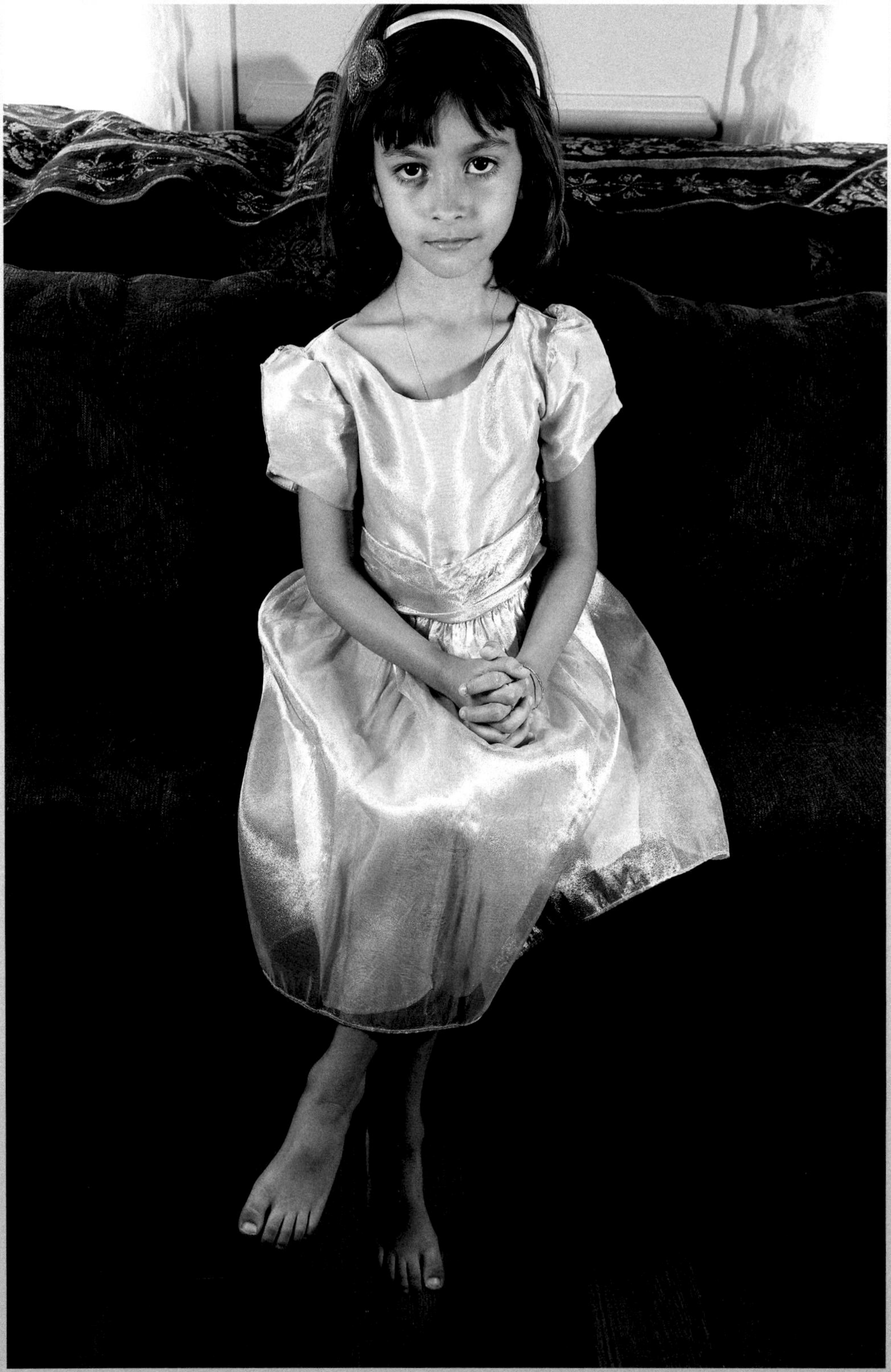

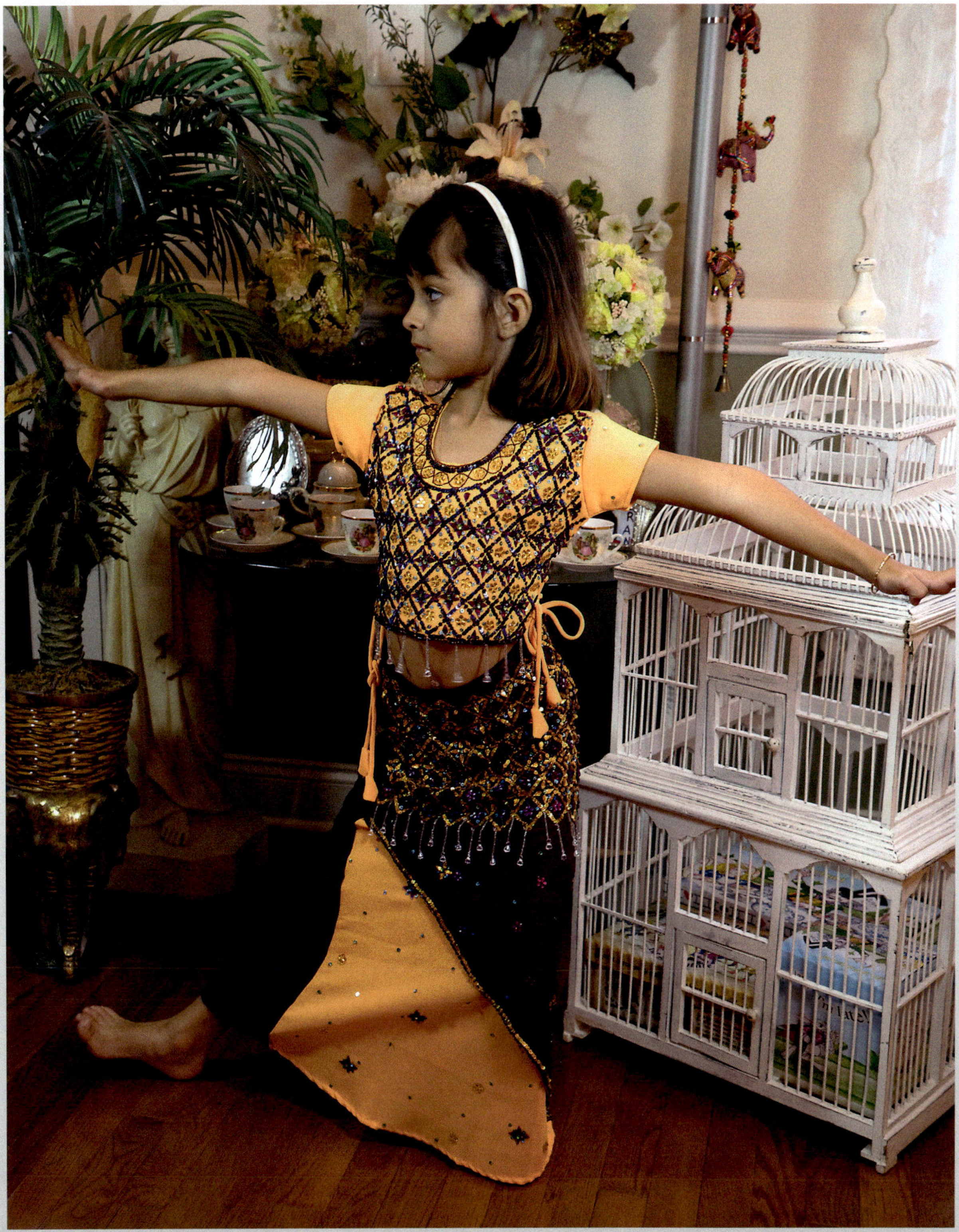

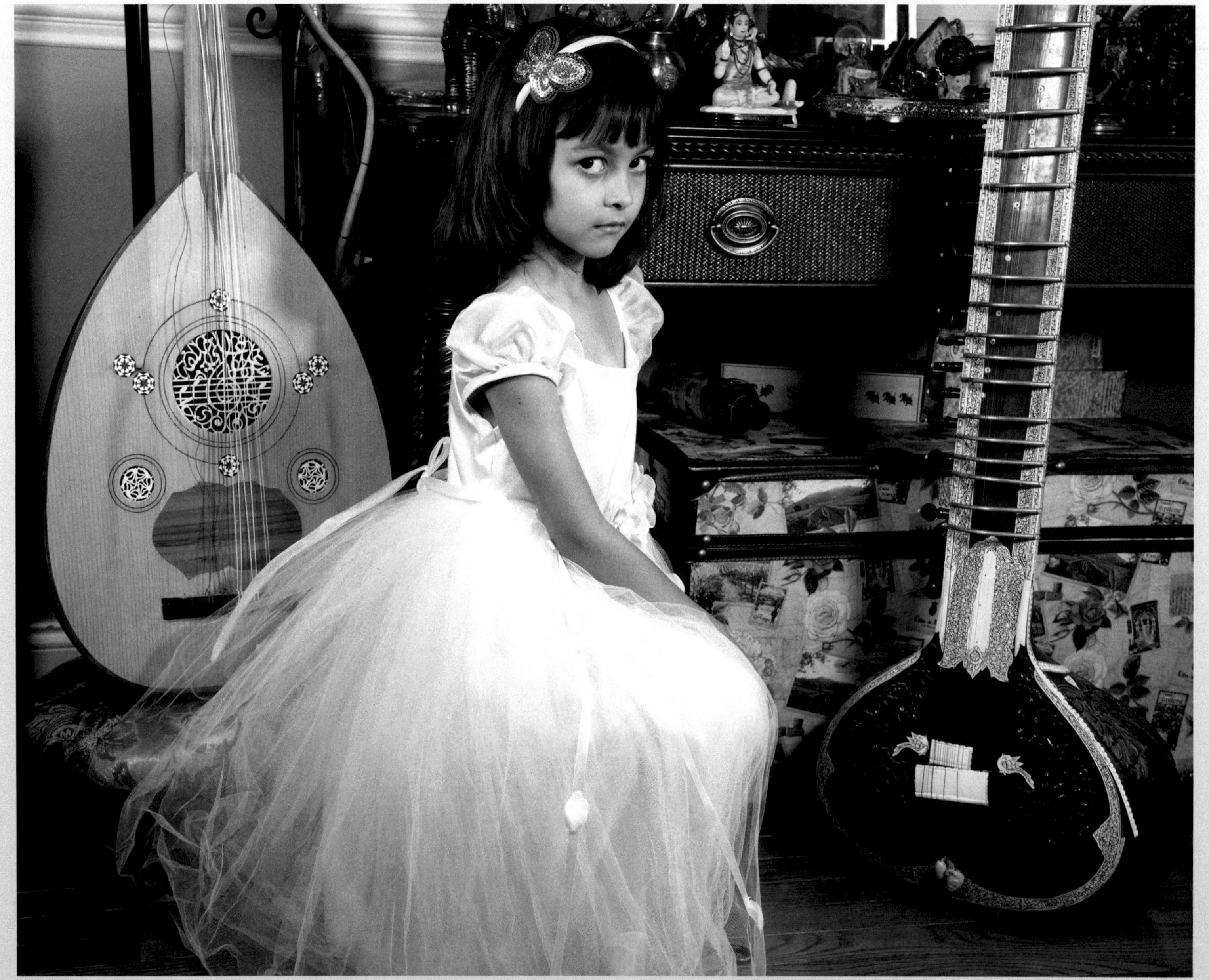

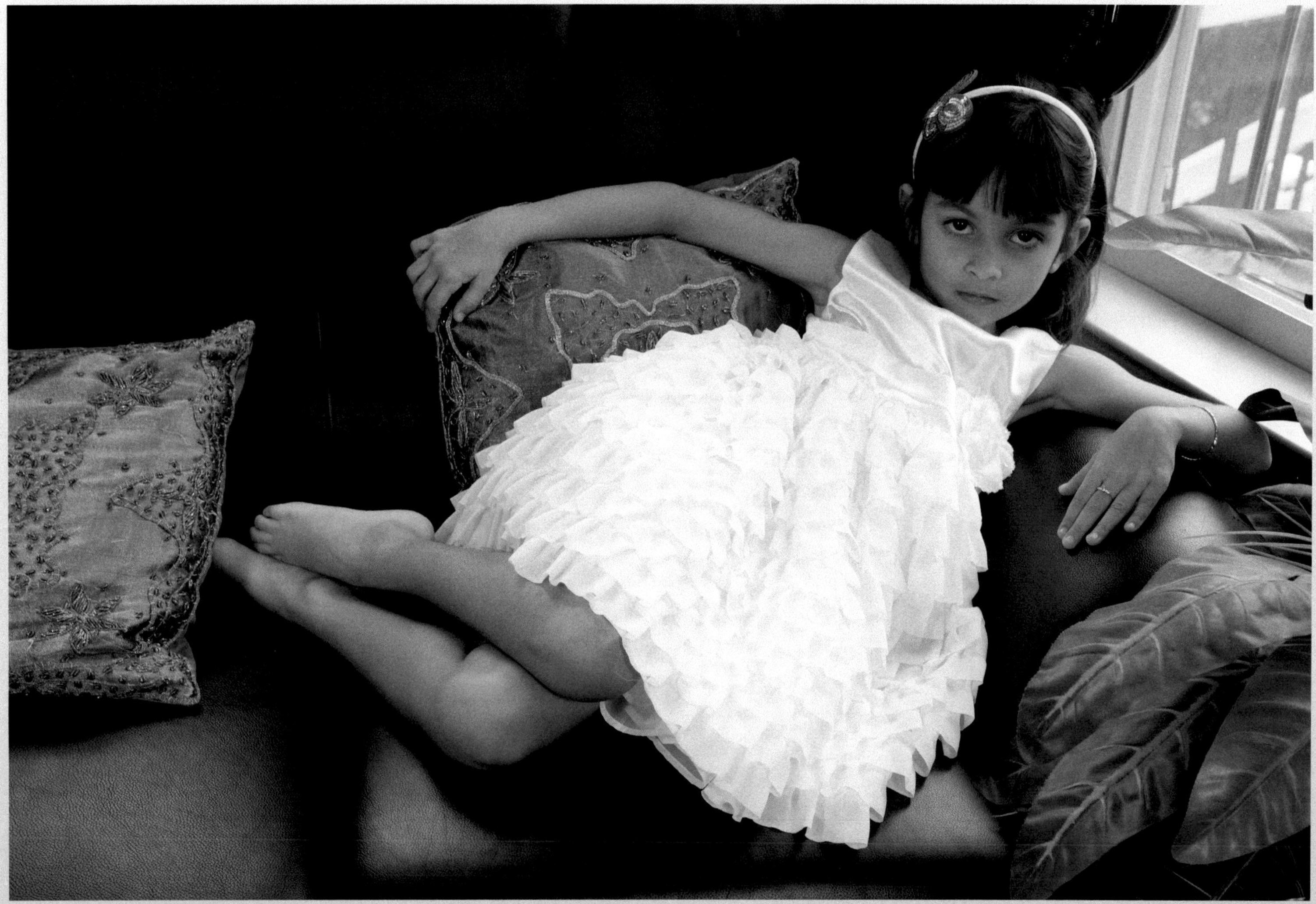

2015/11/02, 4:43:49 pm

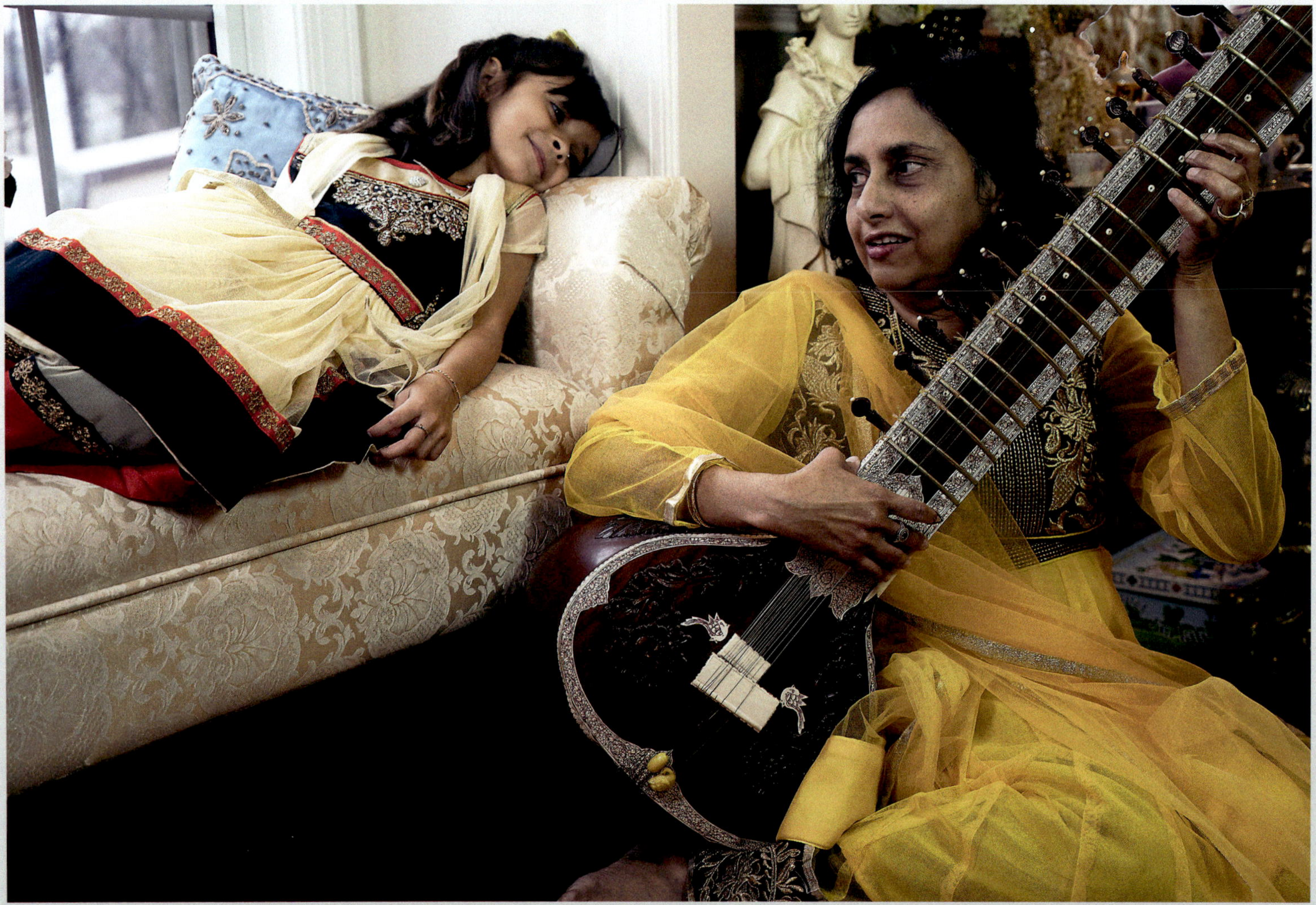

Aryani with Mama and her sitar

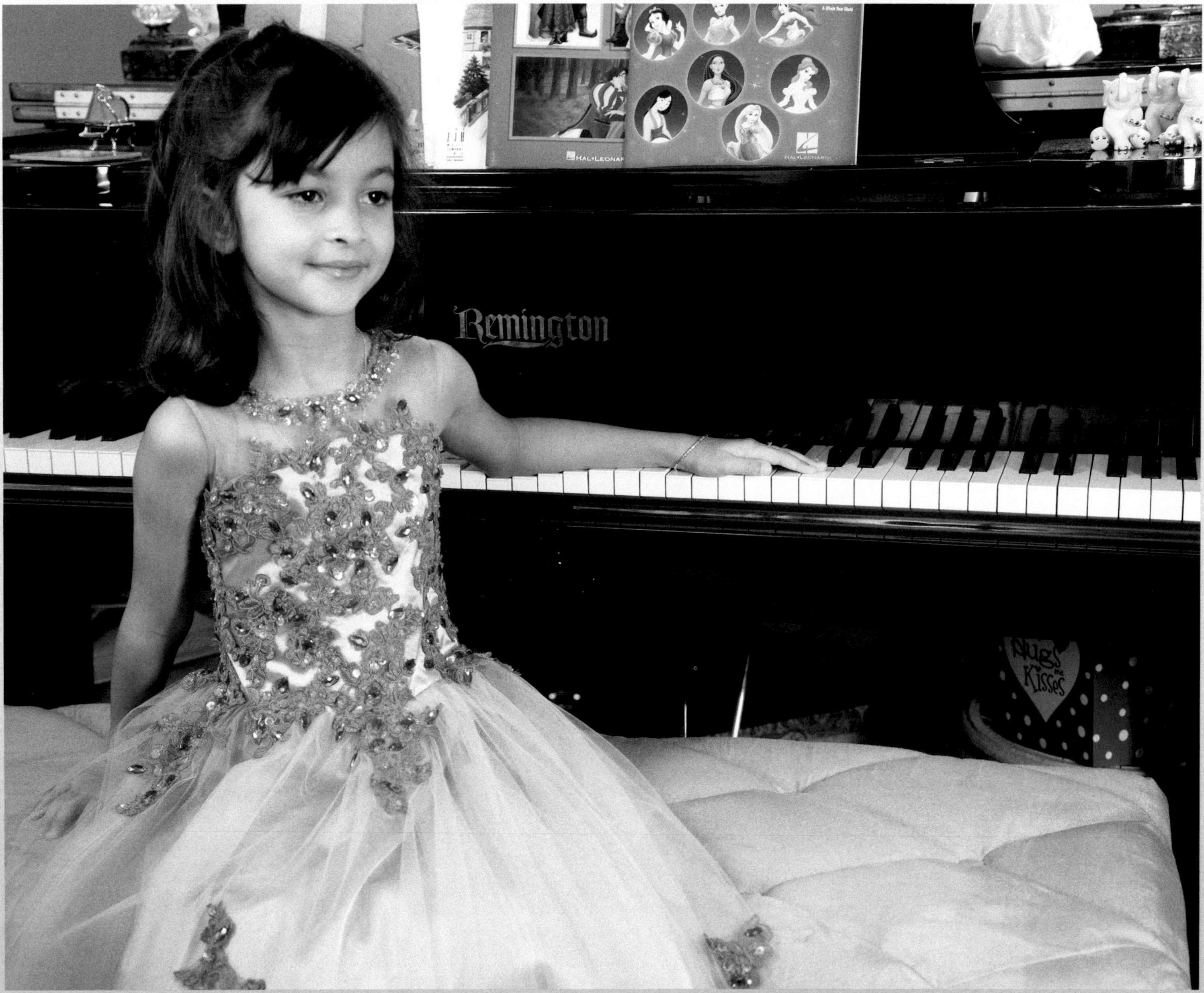


Princesses

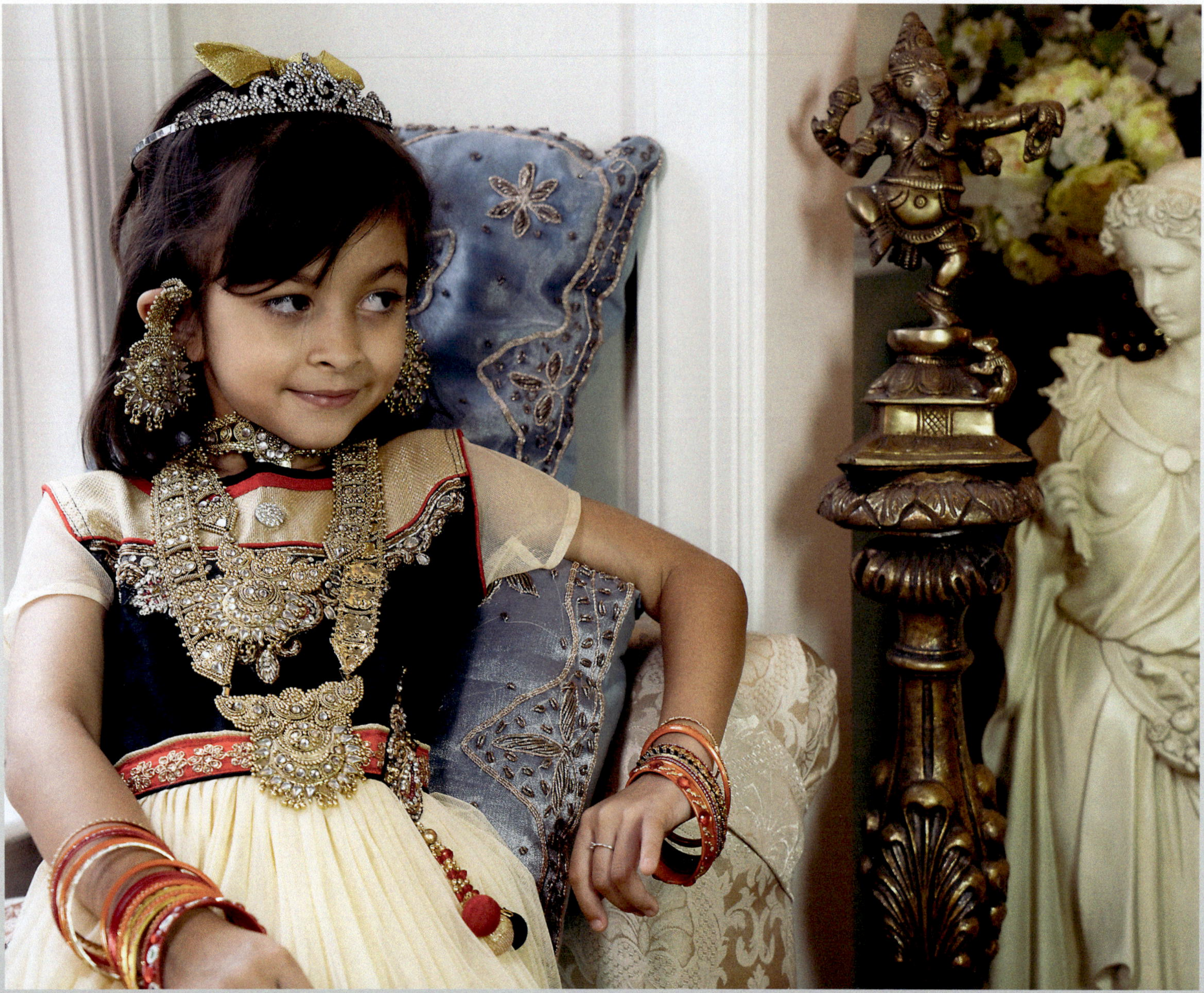

East and West juxtaposed

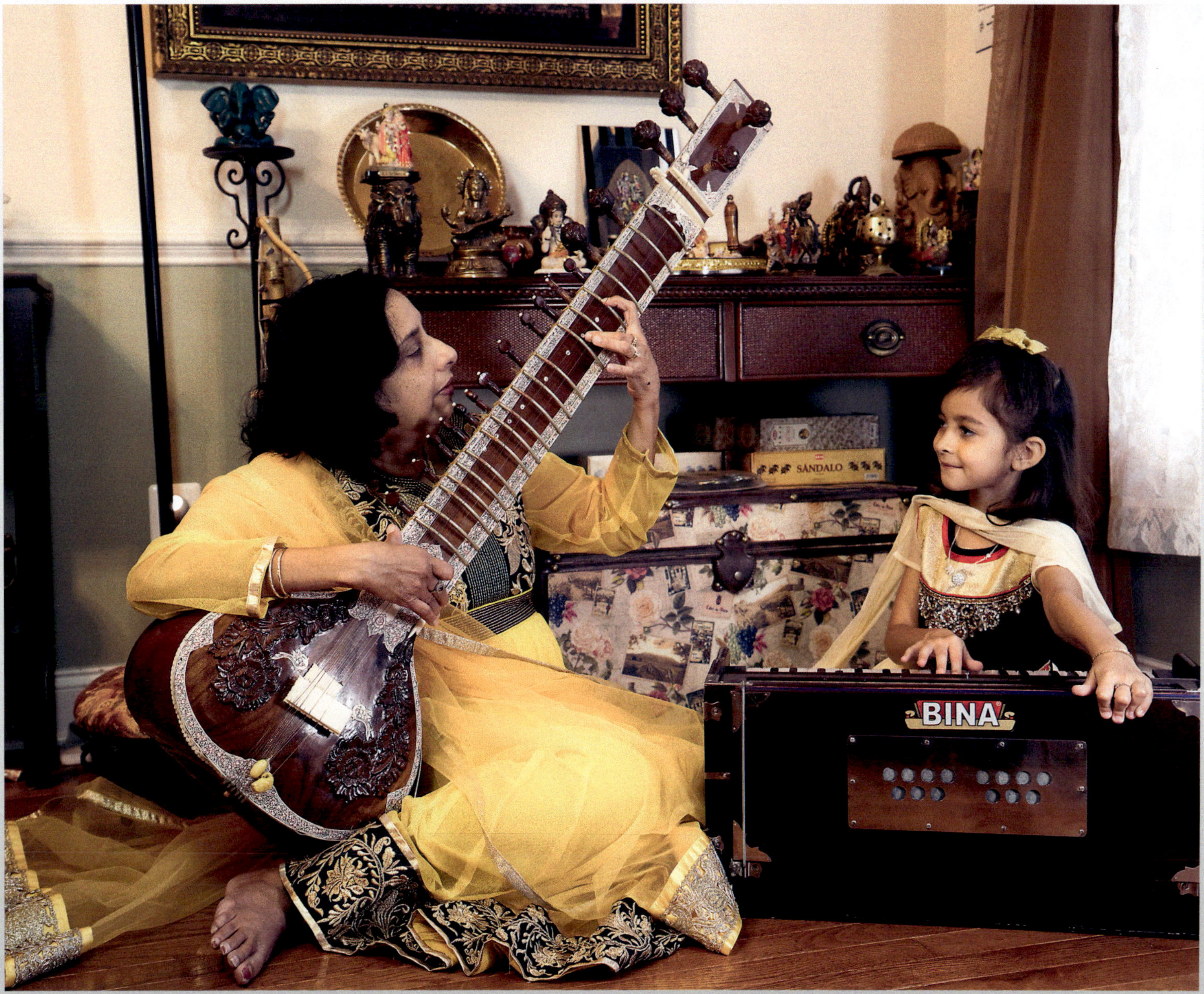


Mama on sitar and Aryani on the harmonium

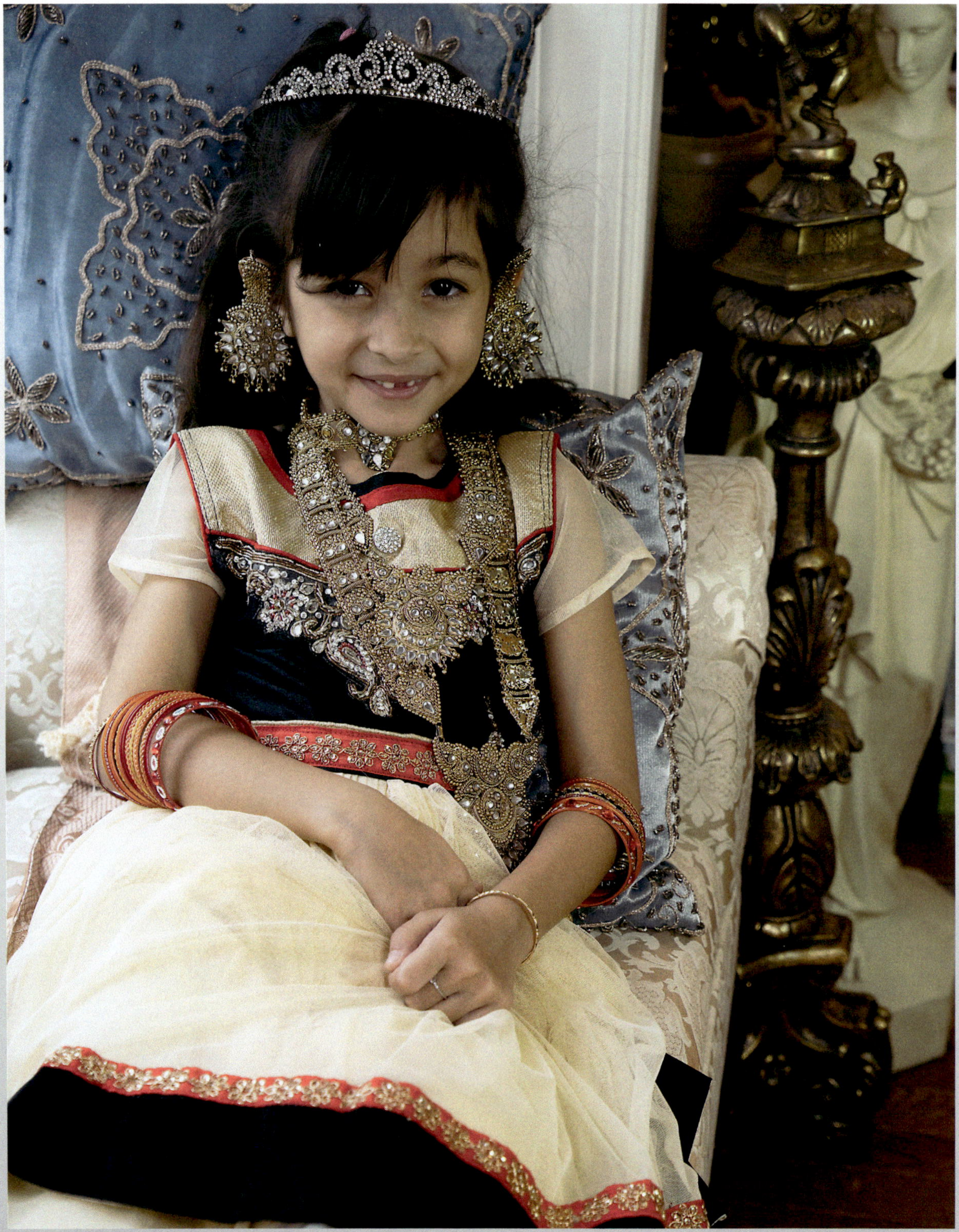


2015/12/22, 2:28:45 pm

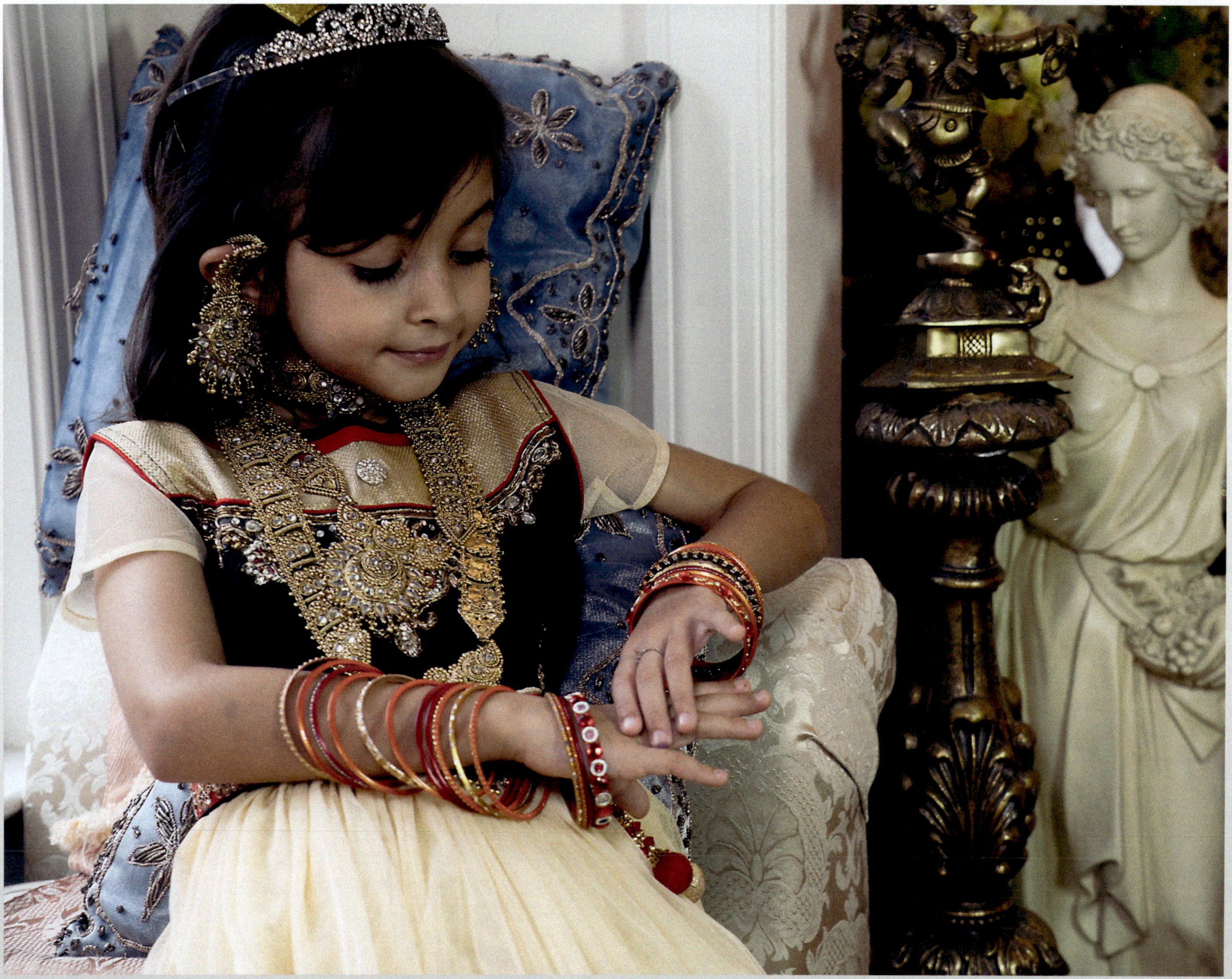

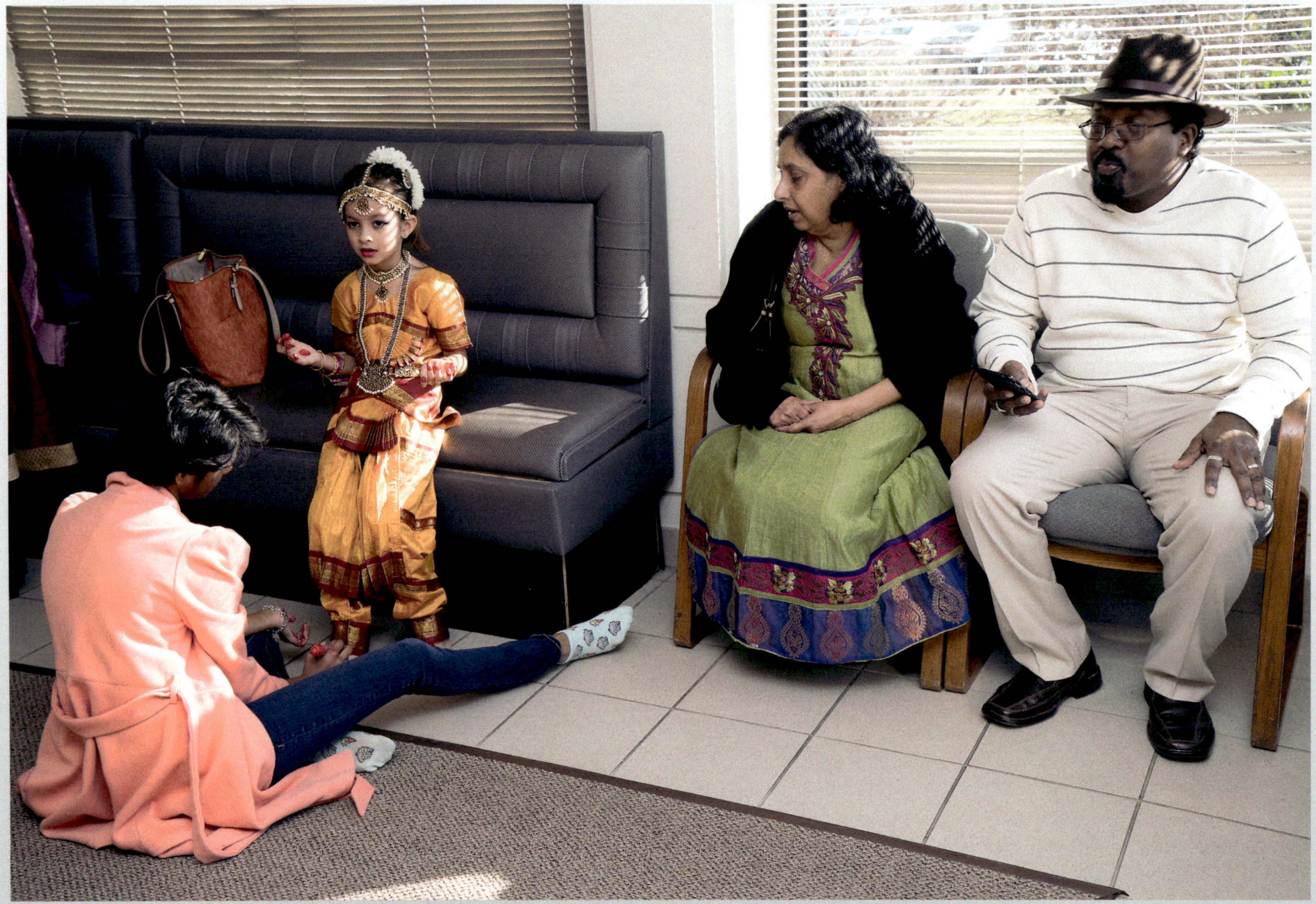

Deshi helping with dance performance preparations with Mama and Nana nearby.



2016/01/16, 11:21:53 am

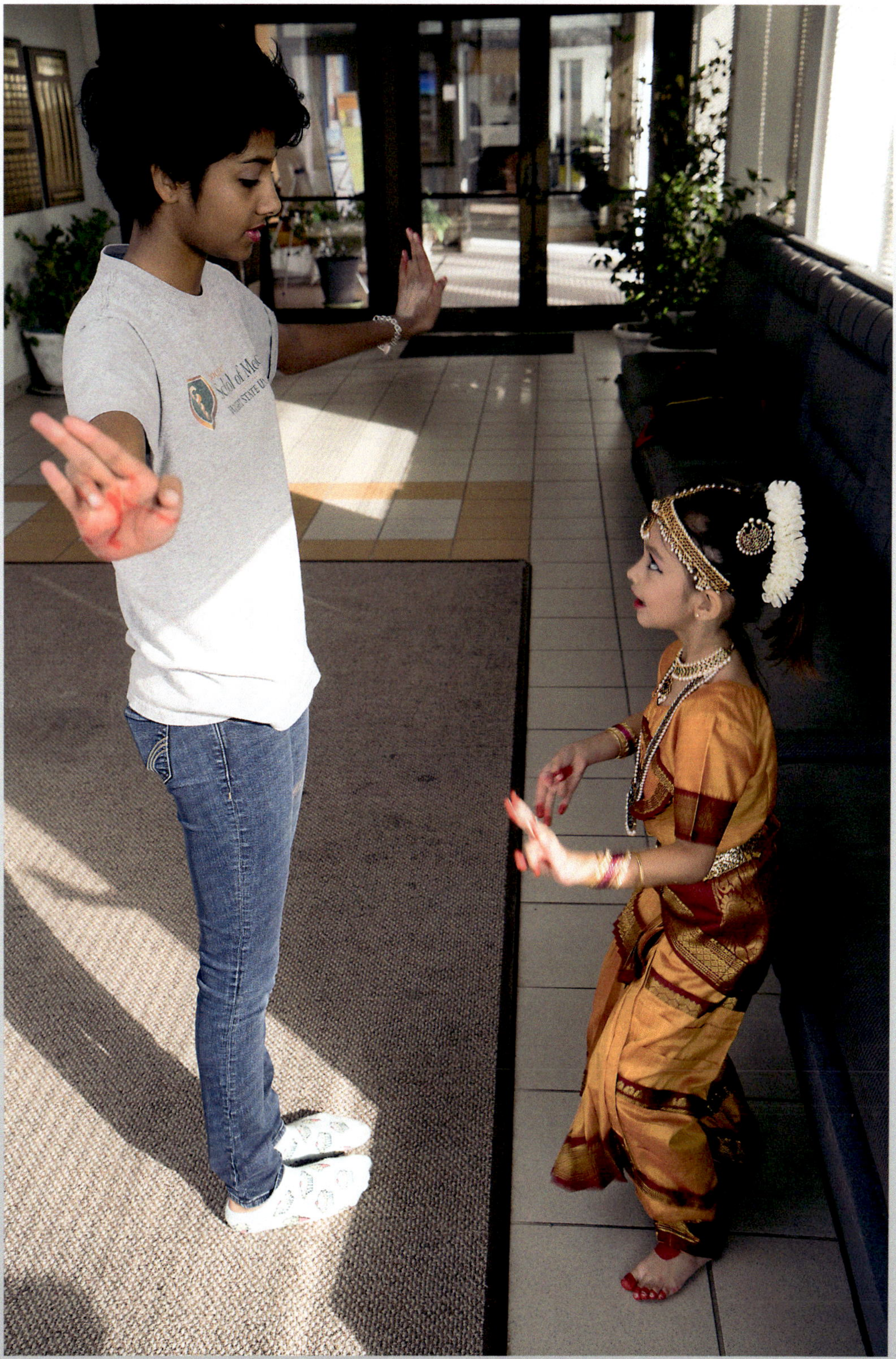

Last minute refresher by Deshi

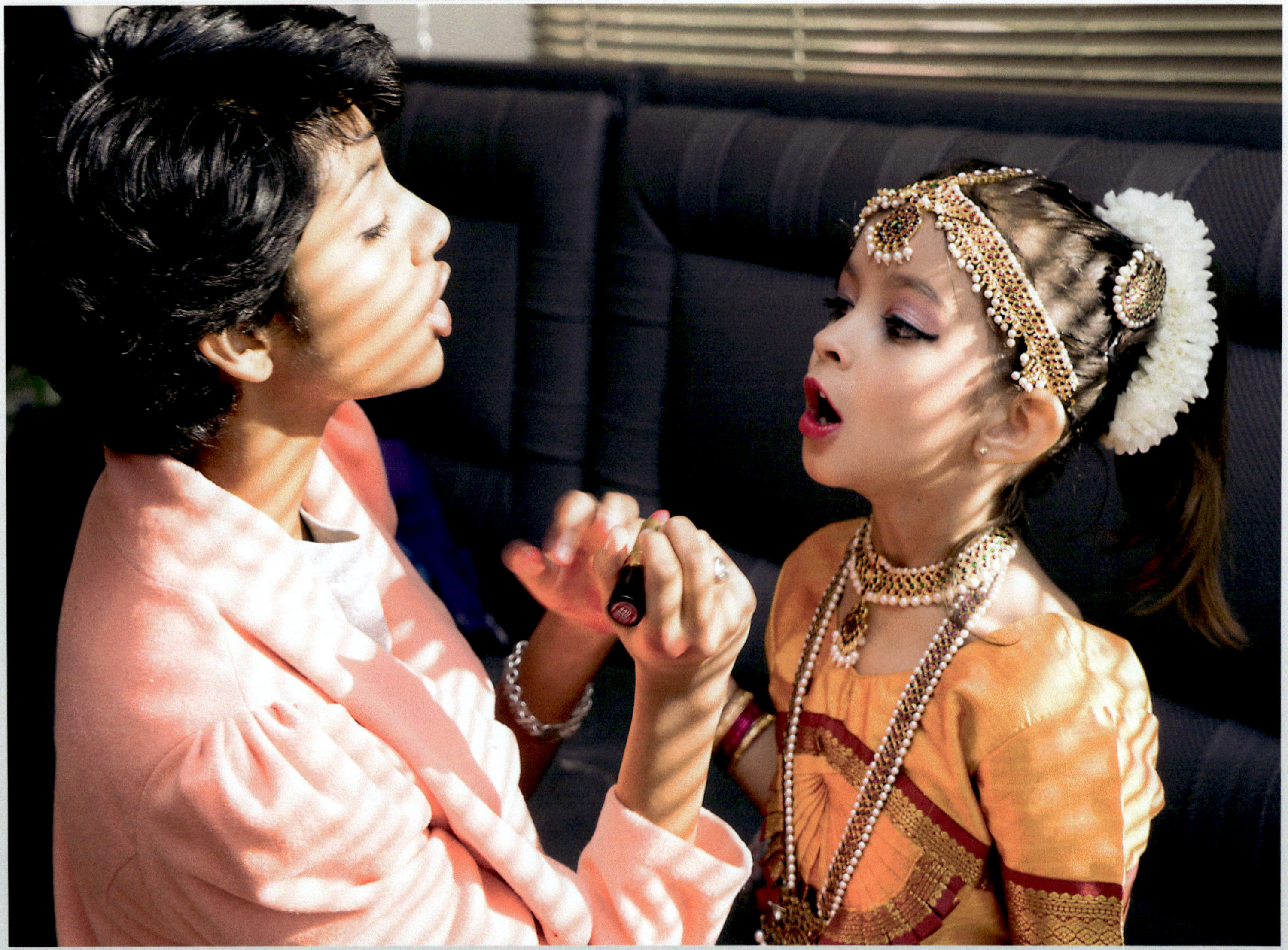

Makup by Deshi



2016/01/16, 11:23:29 am

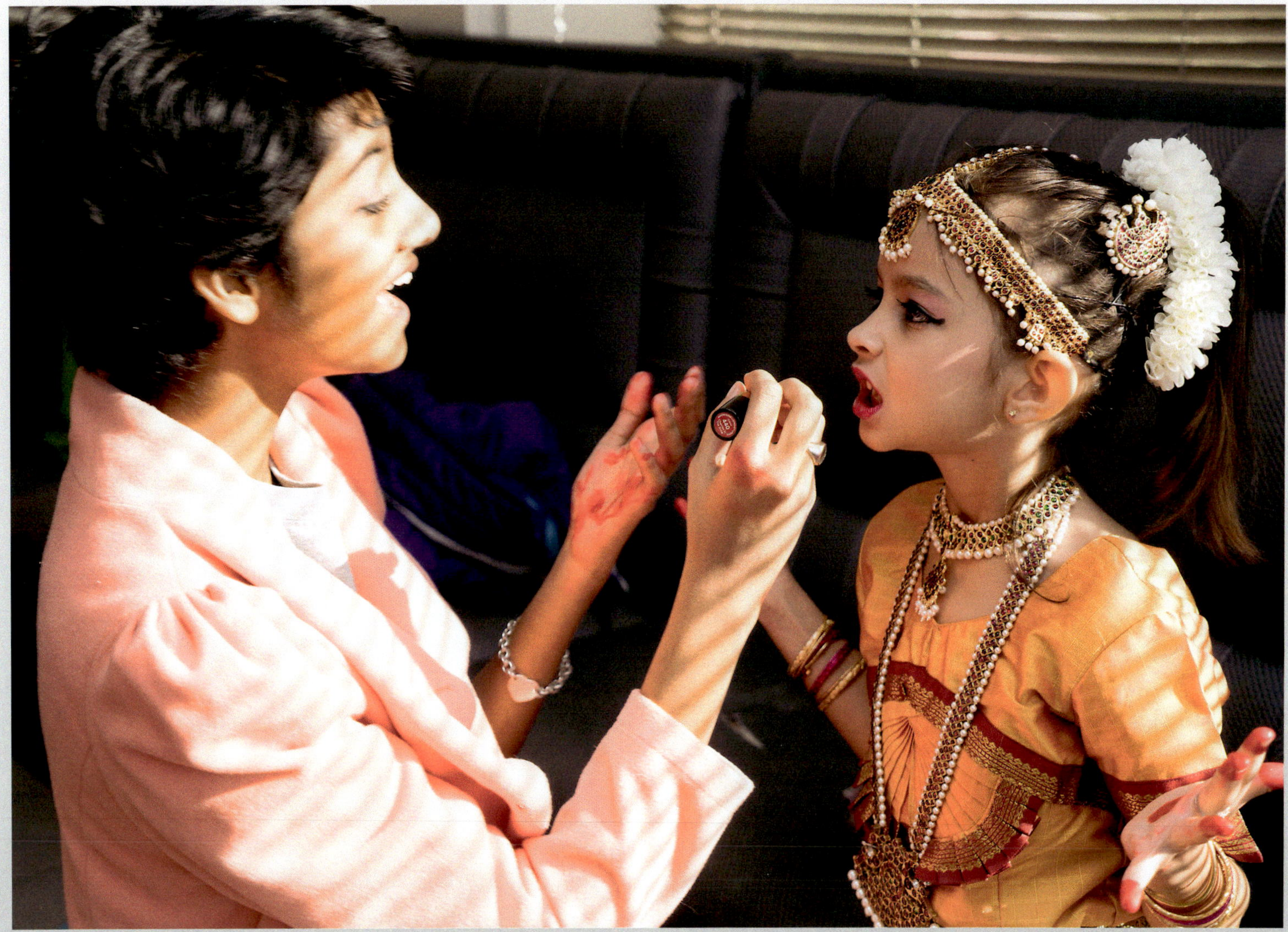

Push back!

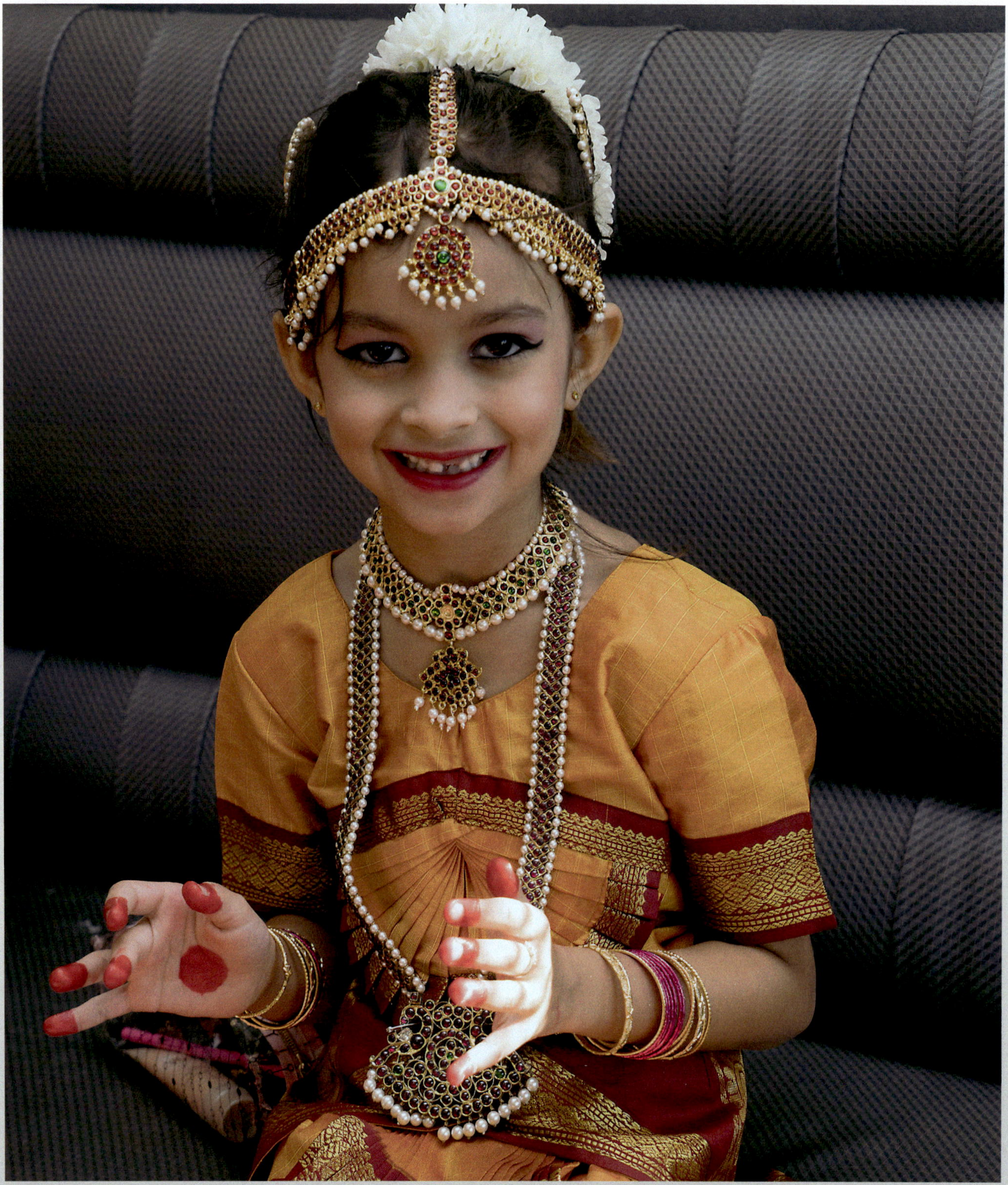

2016/01/16, 11:17:11 am

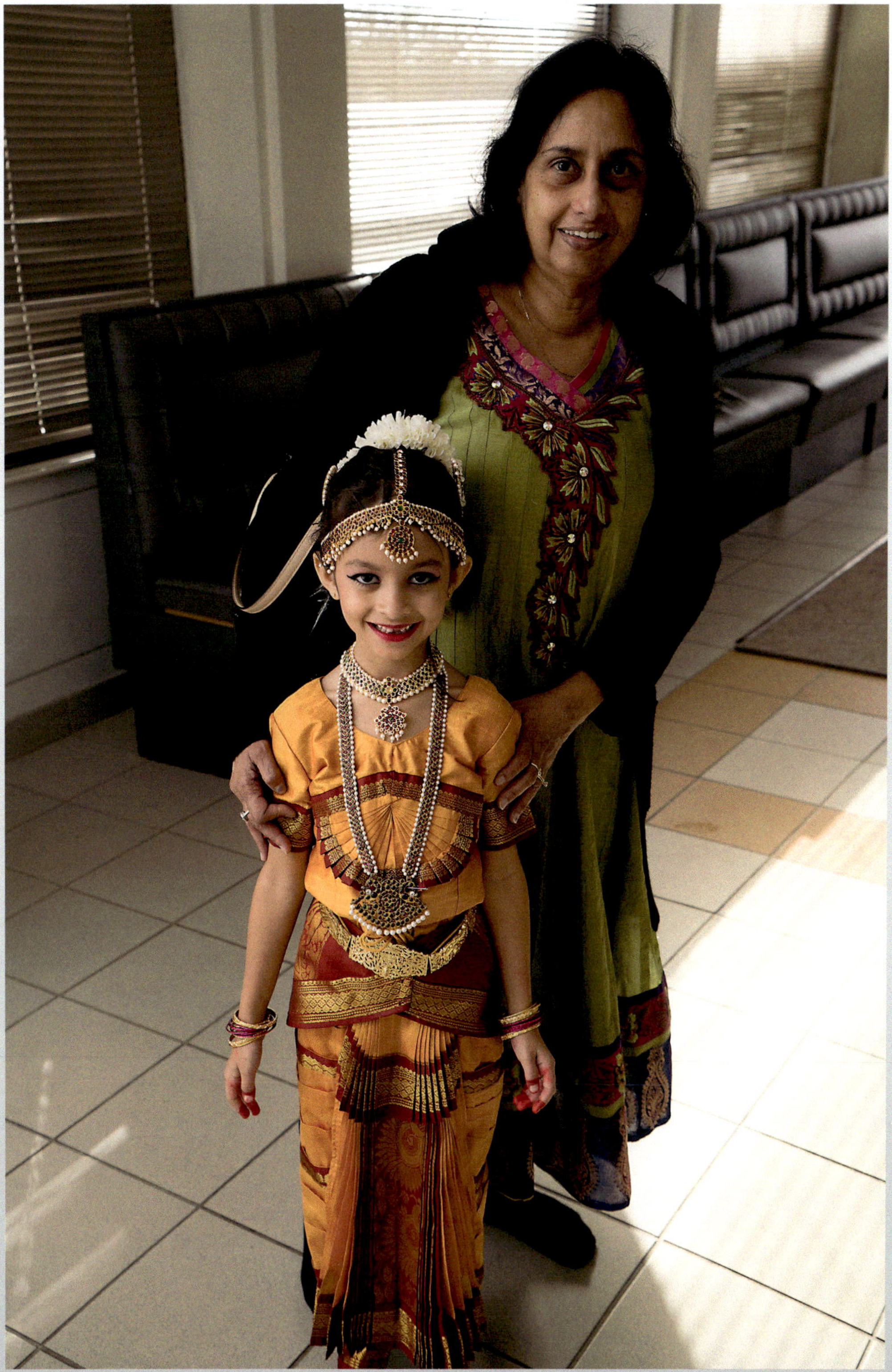

A proud Mama

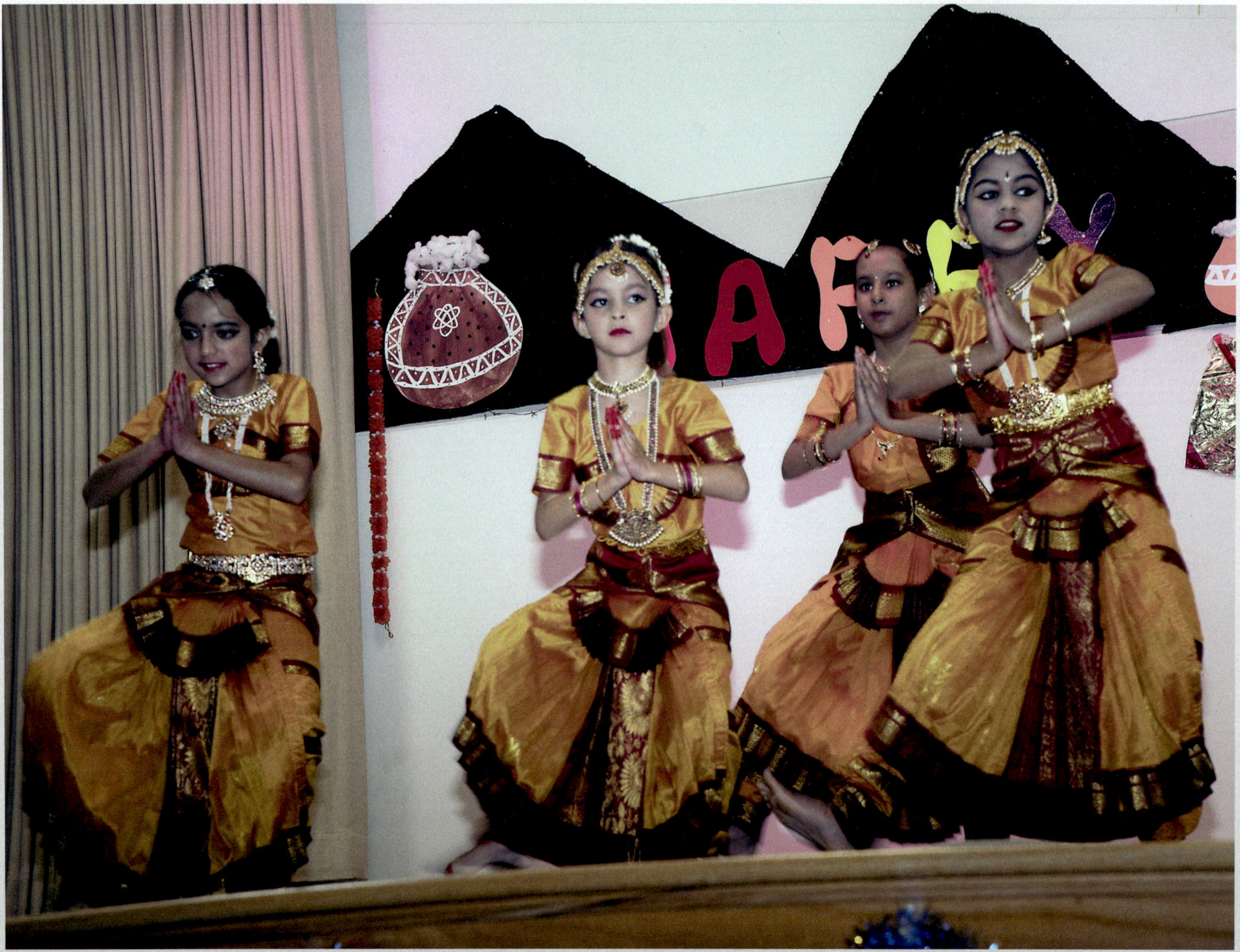

Participating in the Ponga New Year Festival at age six.

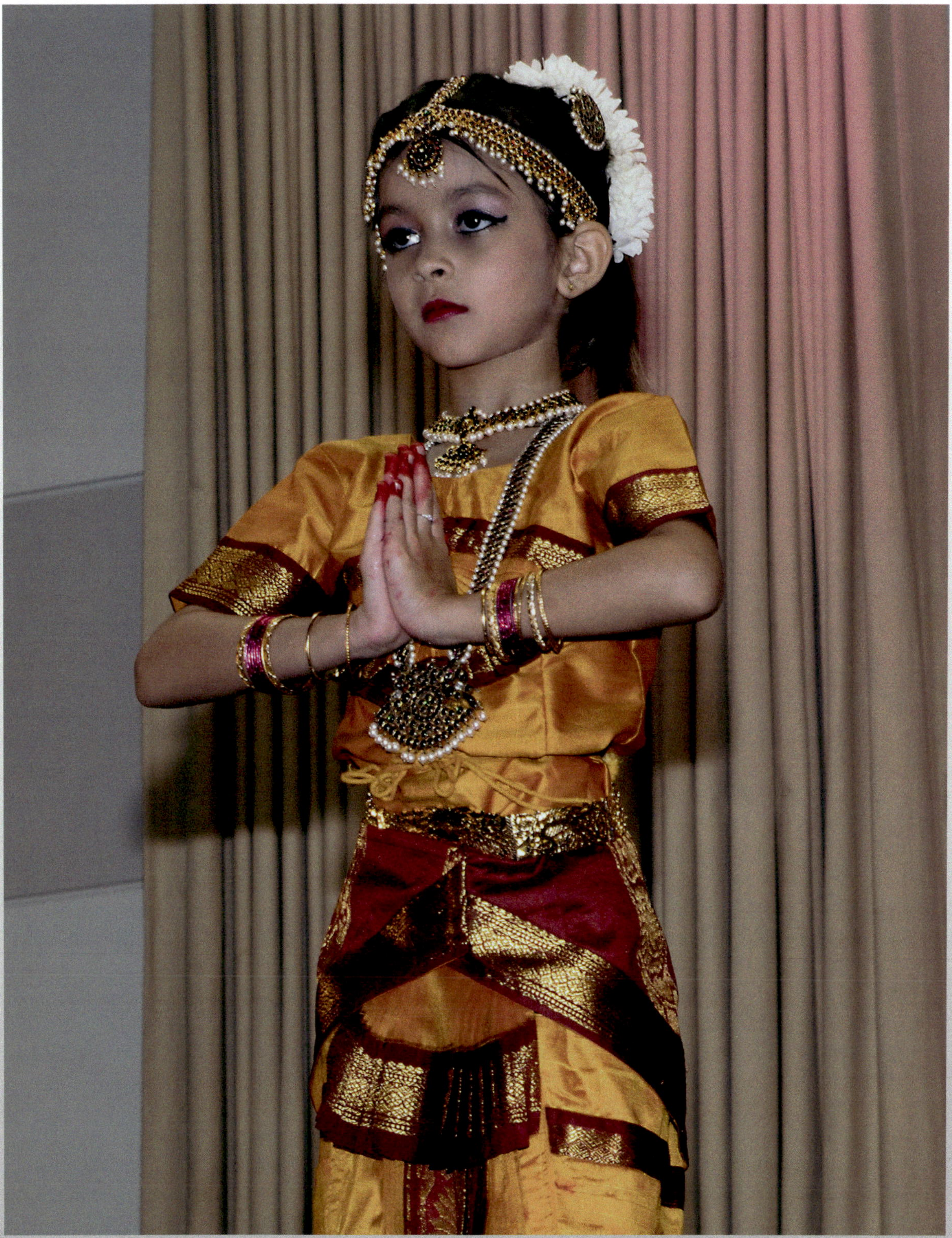

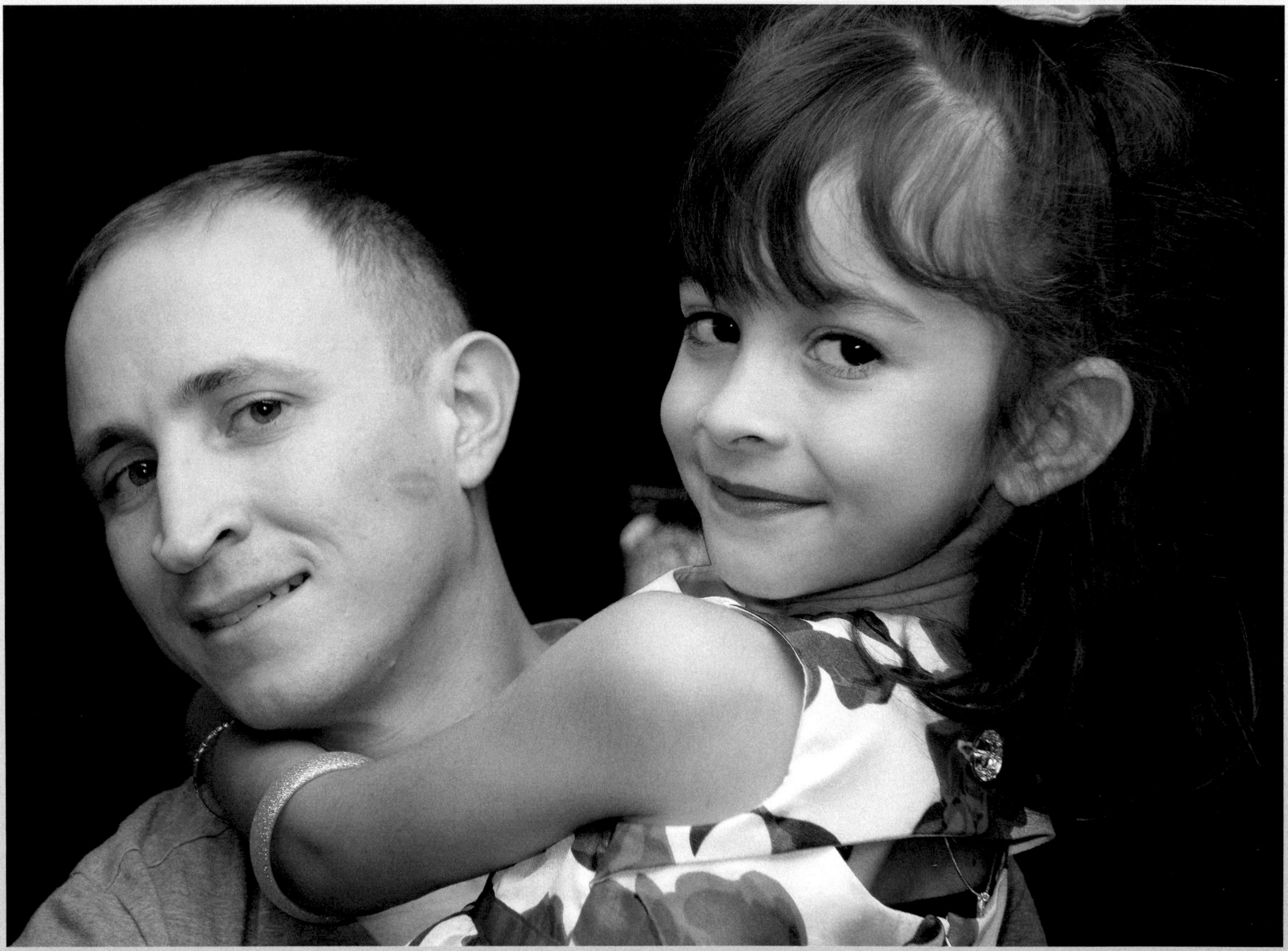

David and the kiss

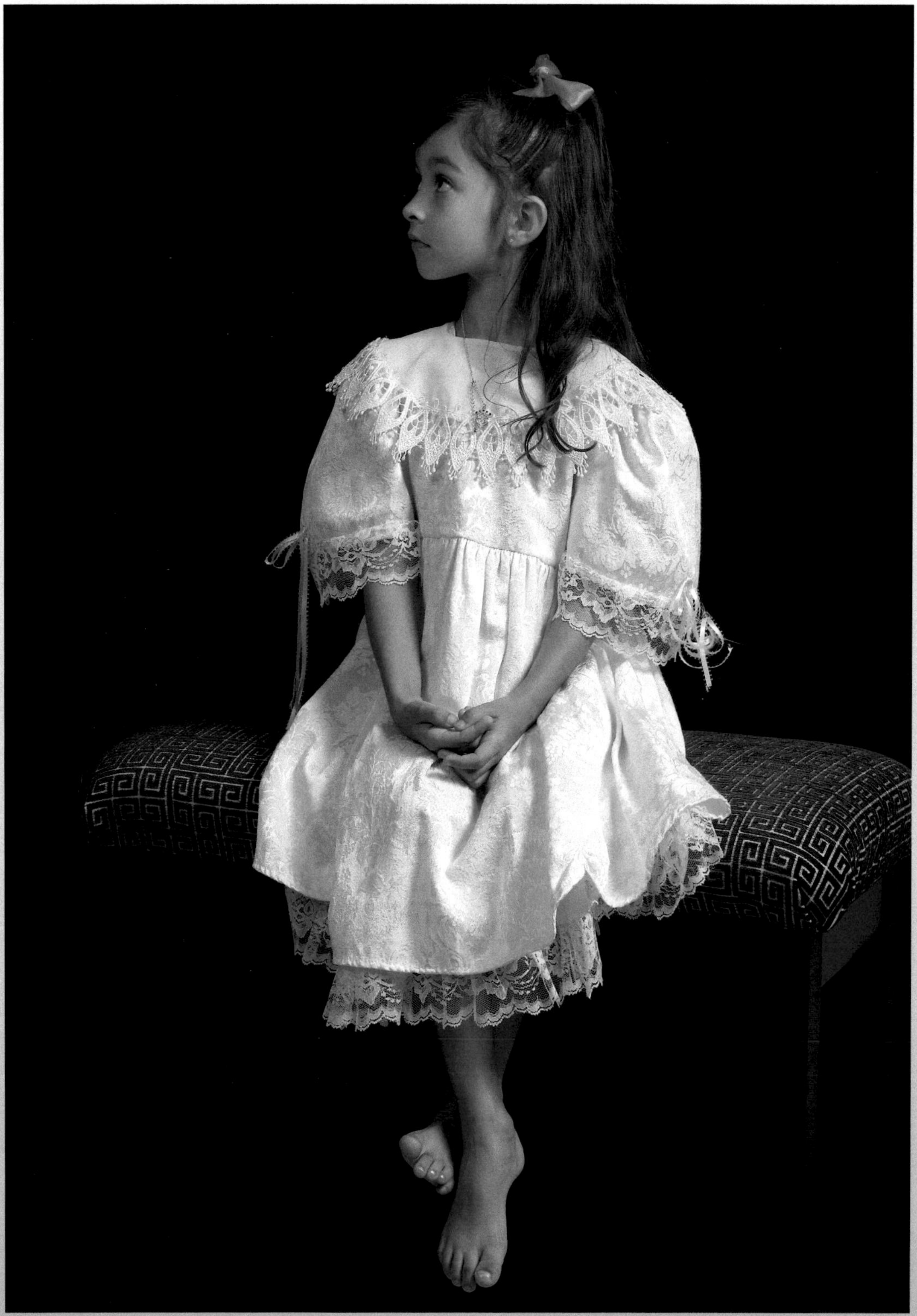

Aryani in Sleepy Mama's dress at age seven

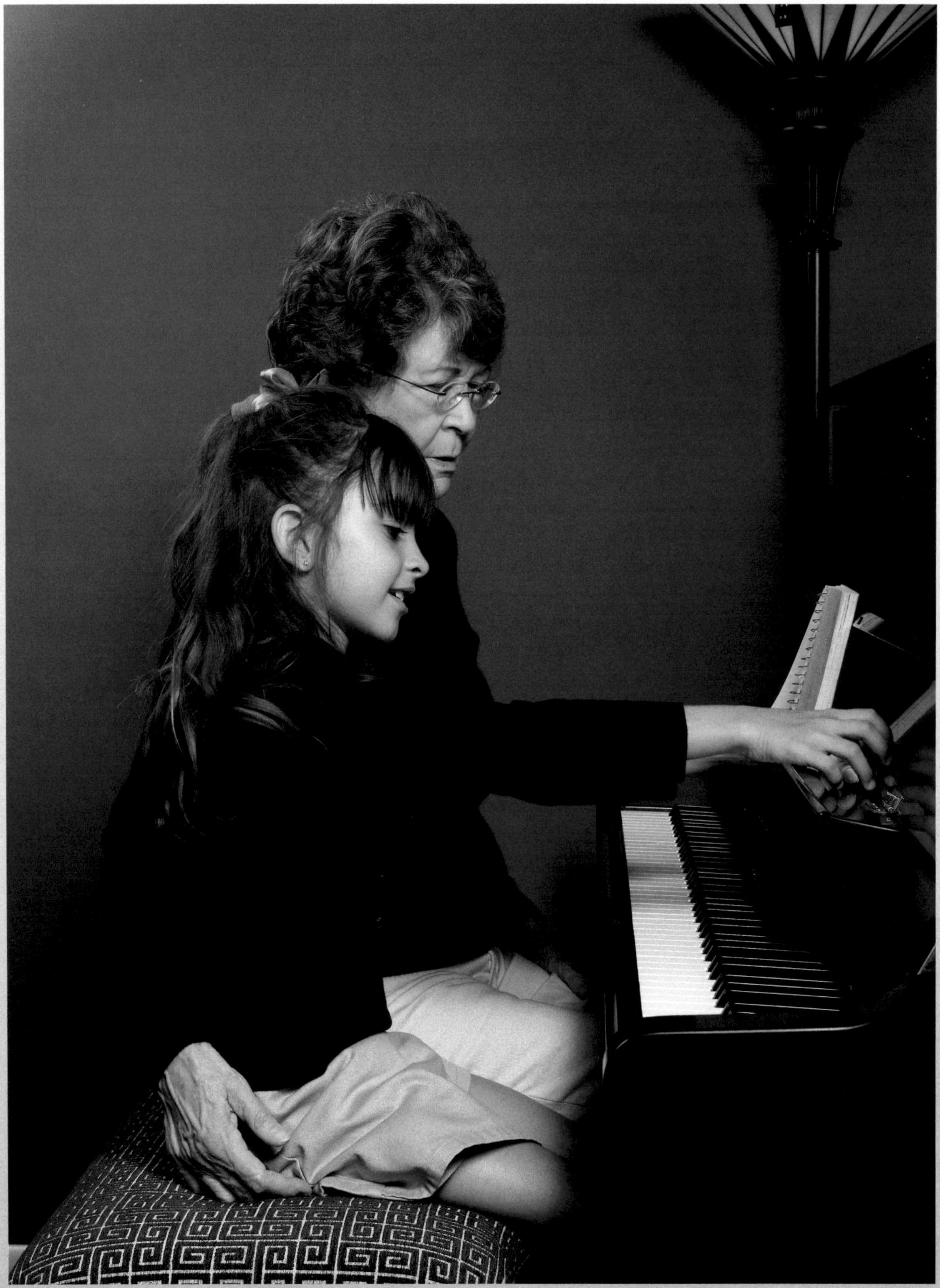

Playing four-hands piano with Grandma Gail

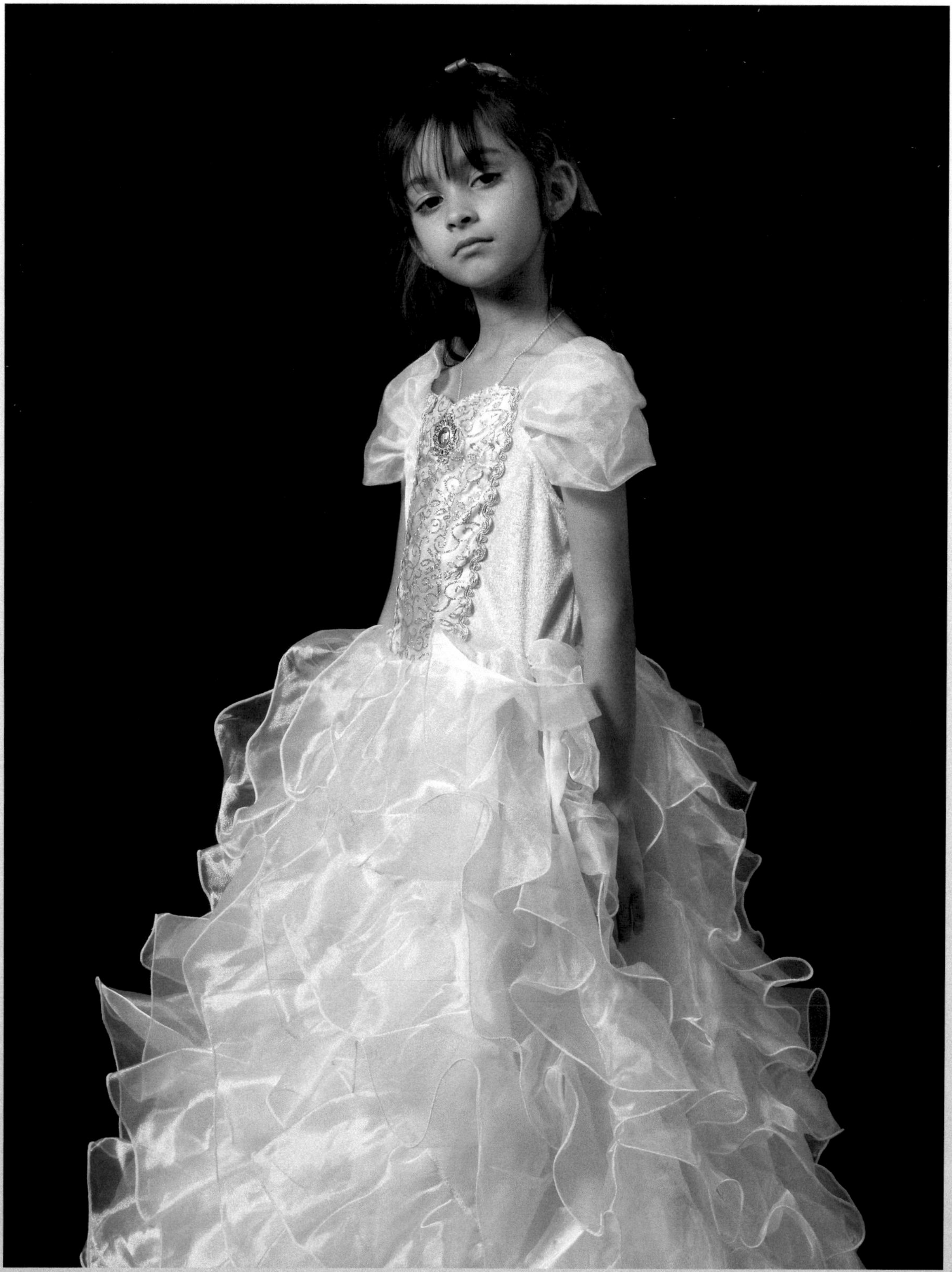

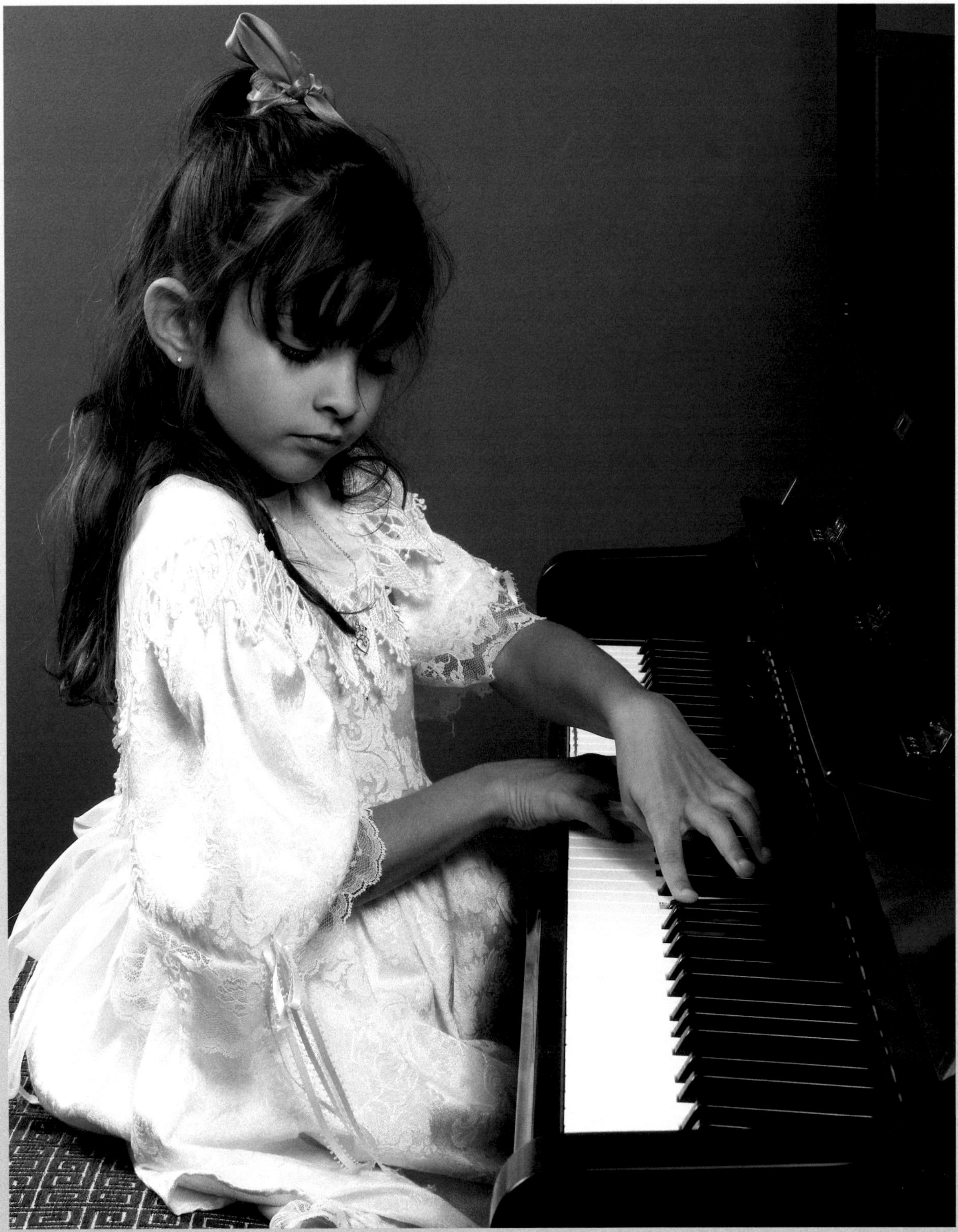

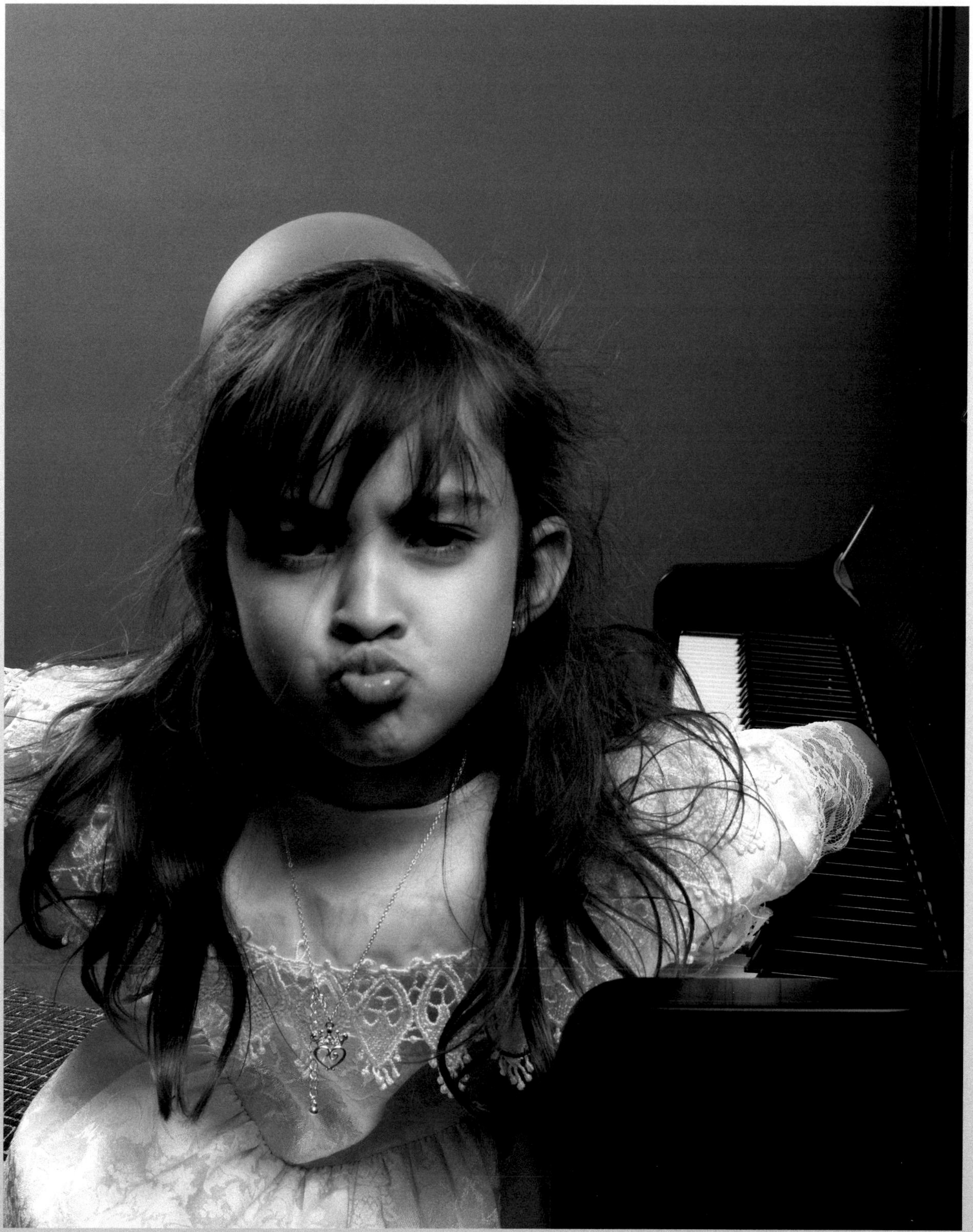

Piano break

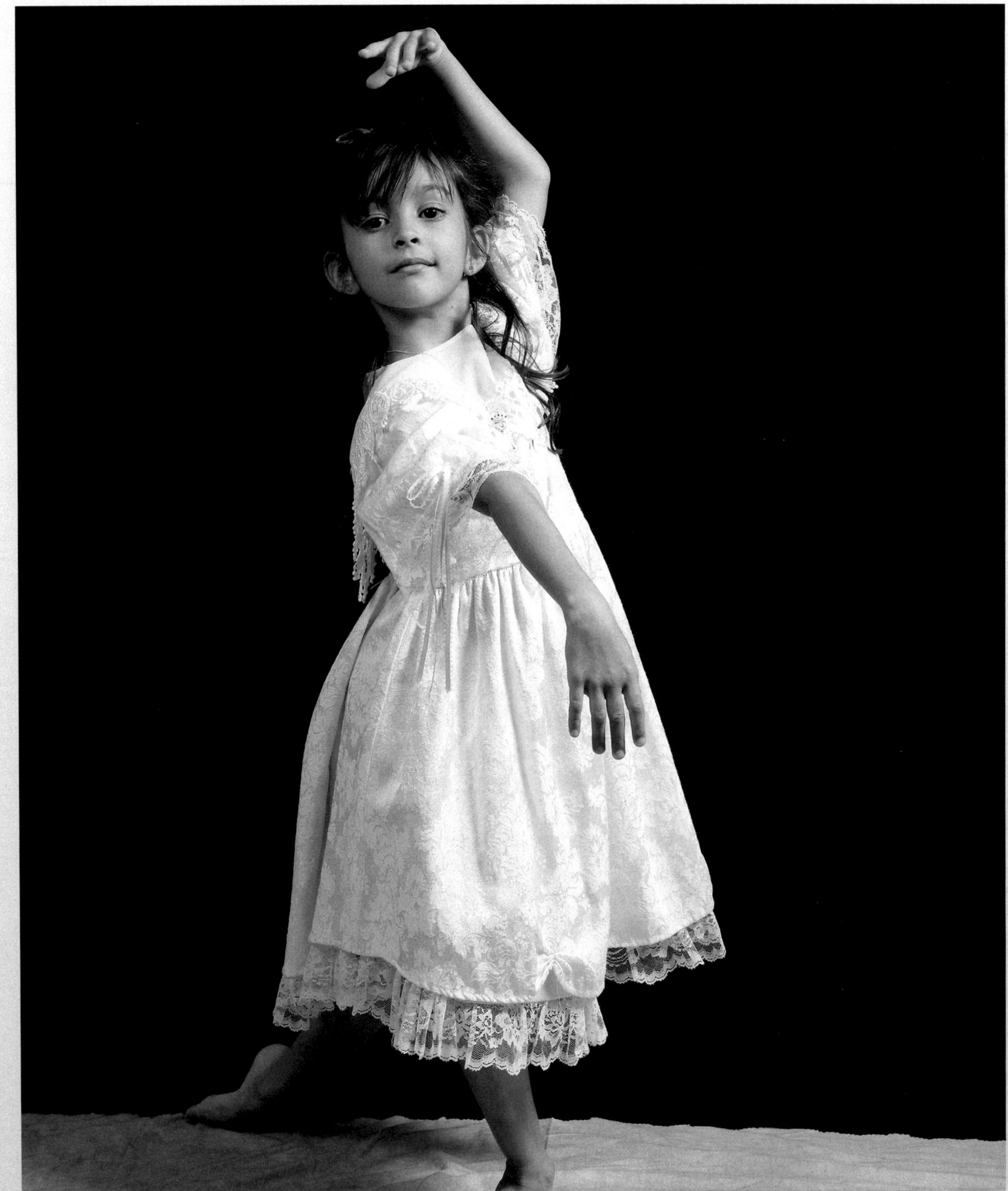

Ballet pose

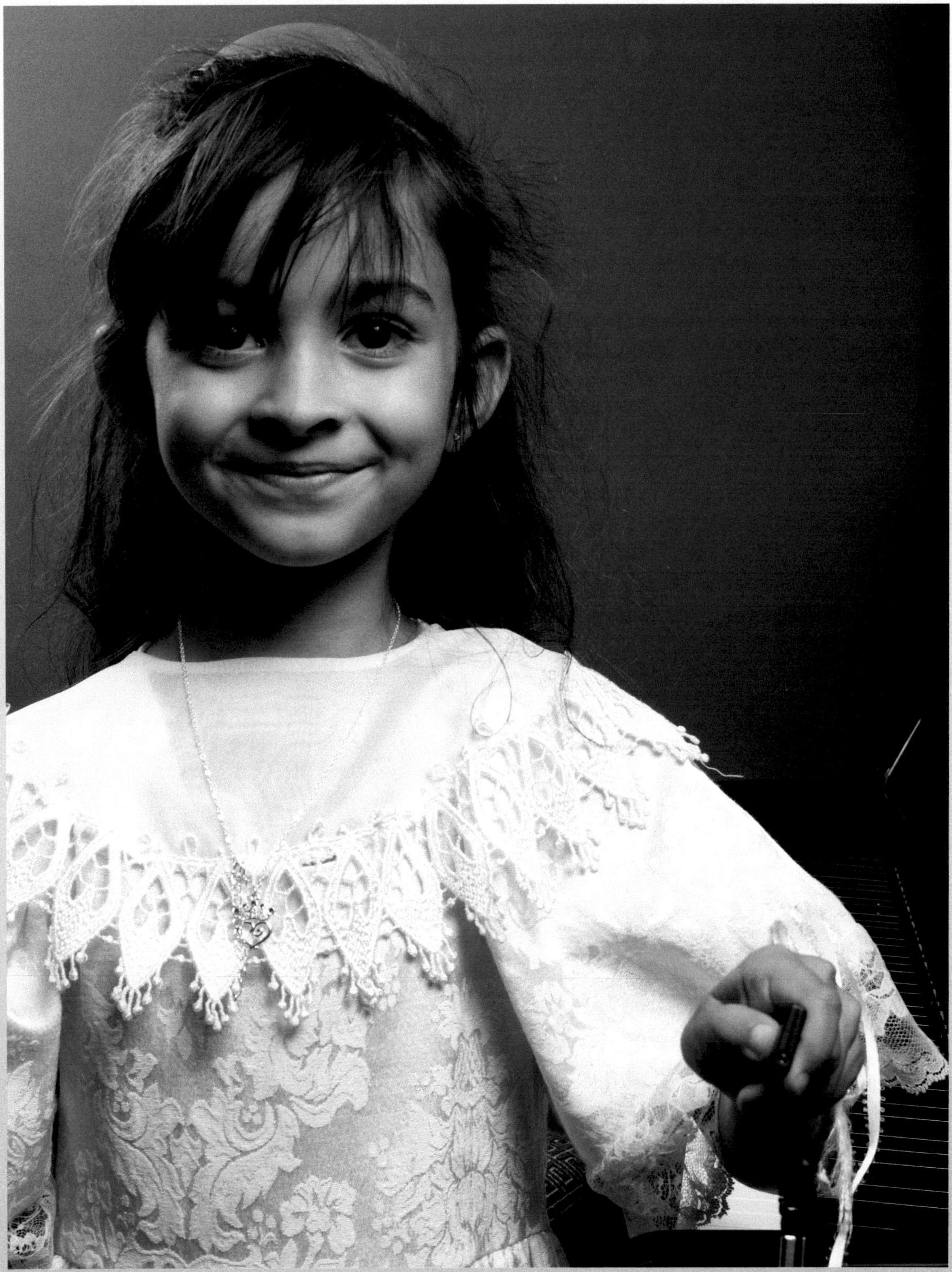

Aryani now master of the camera remote control.

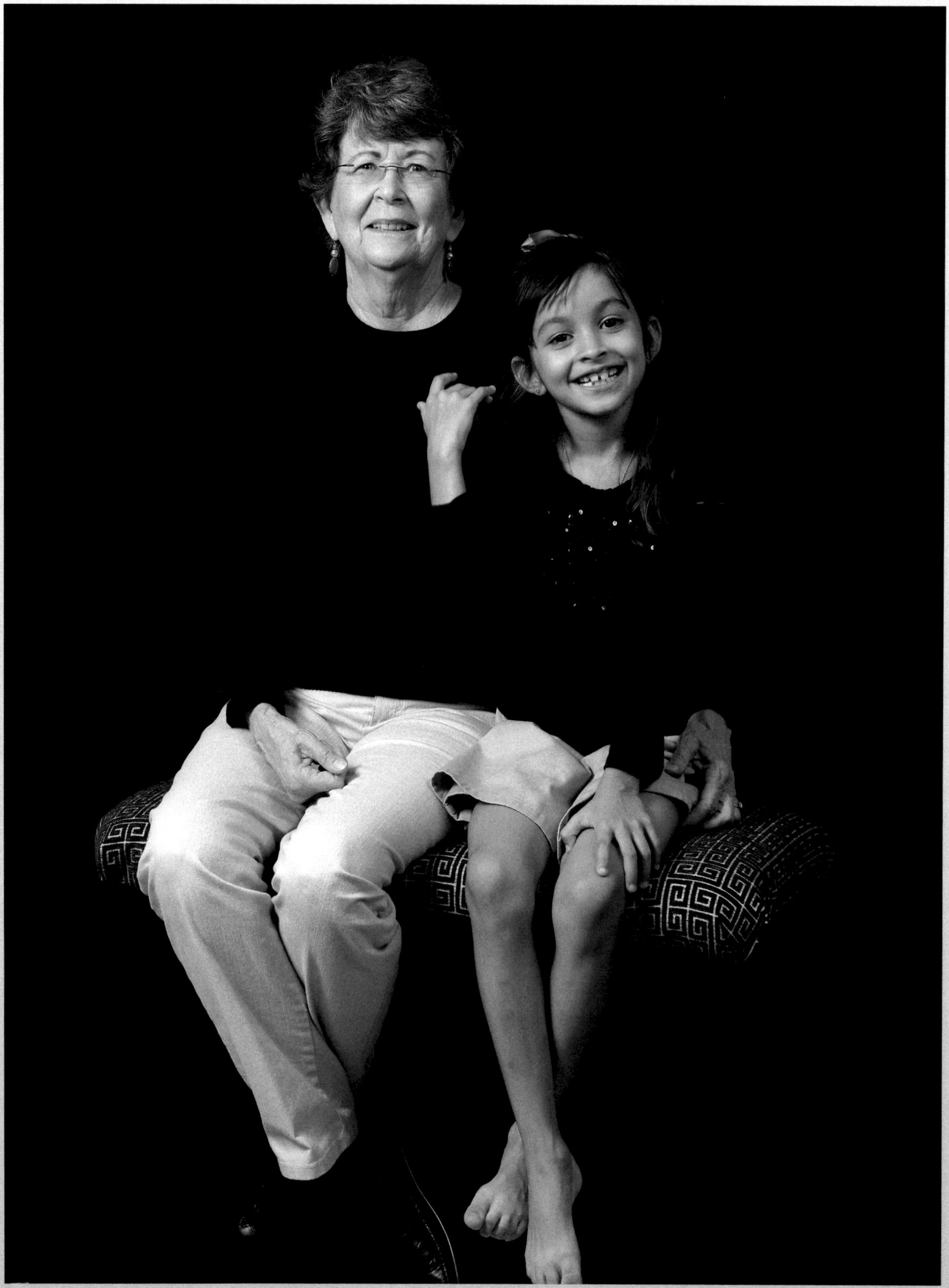

Happy Grandma and granddaughter

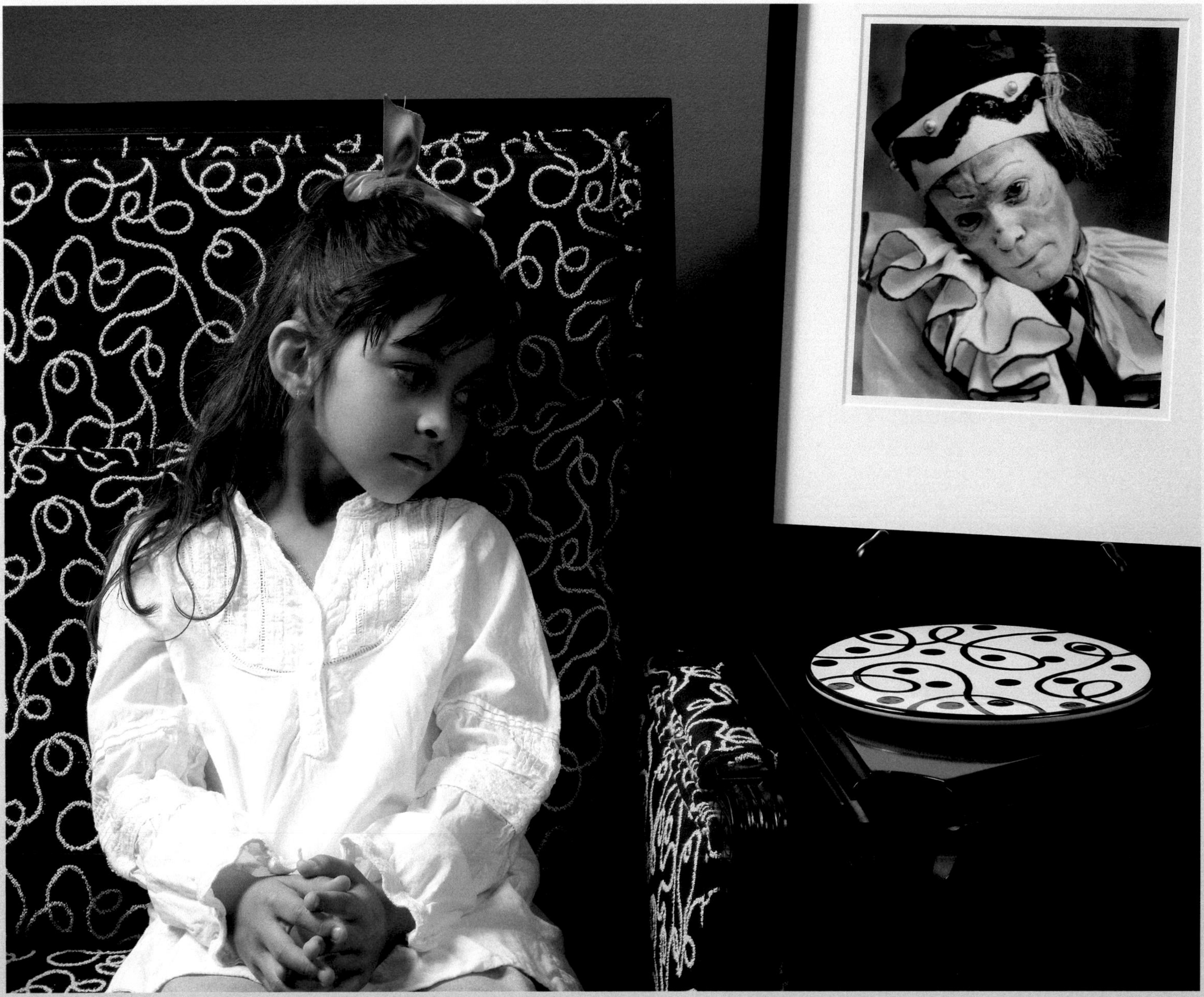

Dual sitting with Vaslav Nijinsky from Stravinsky's 1911 performance of Petrushka

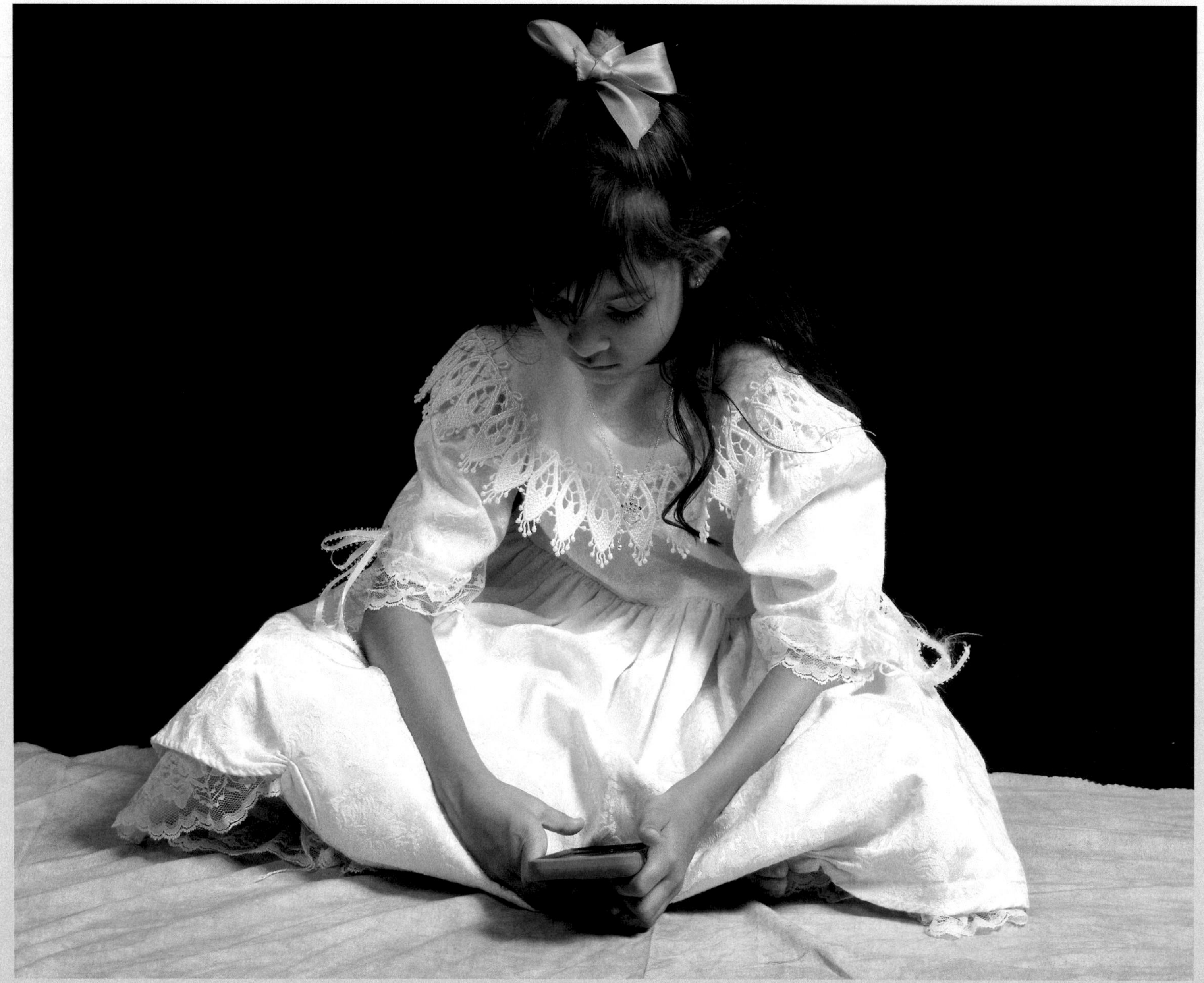

Aryani on break. (Martin was not.)

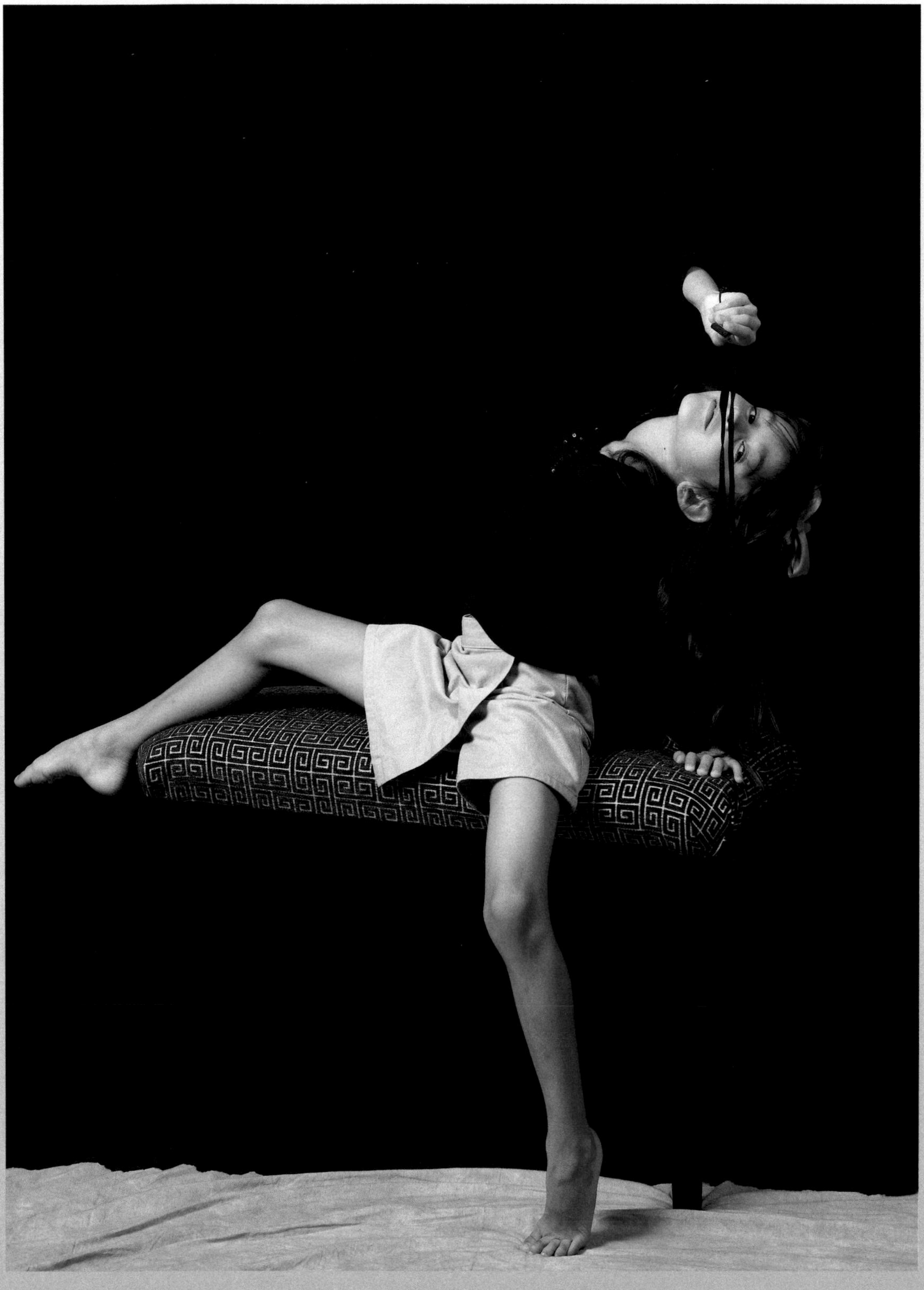

Hamming with the camera remote again!

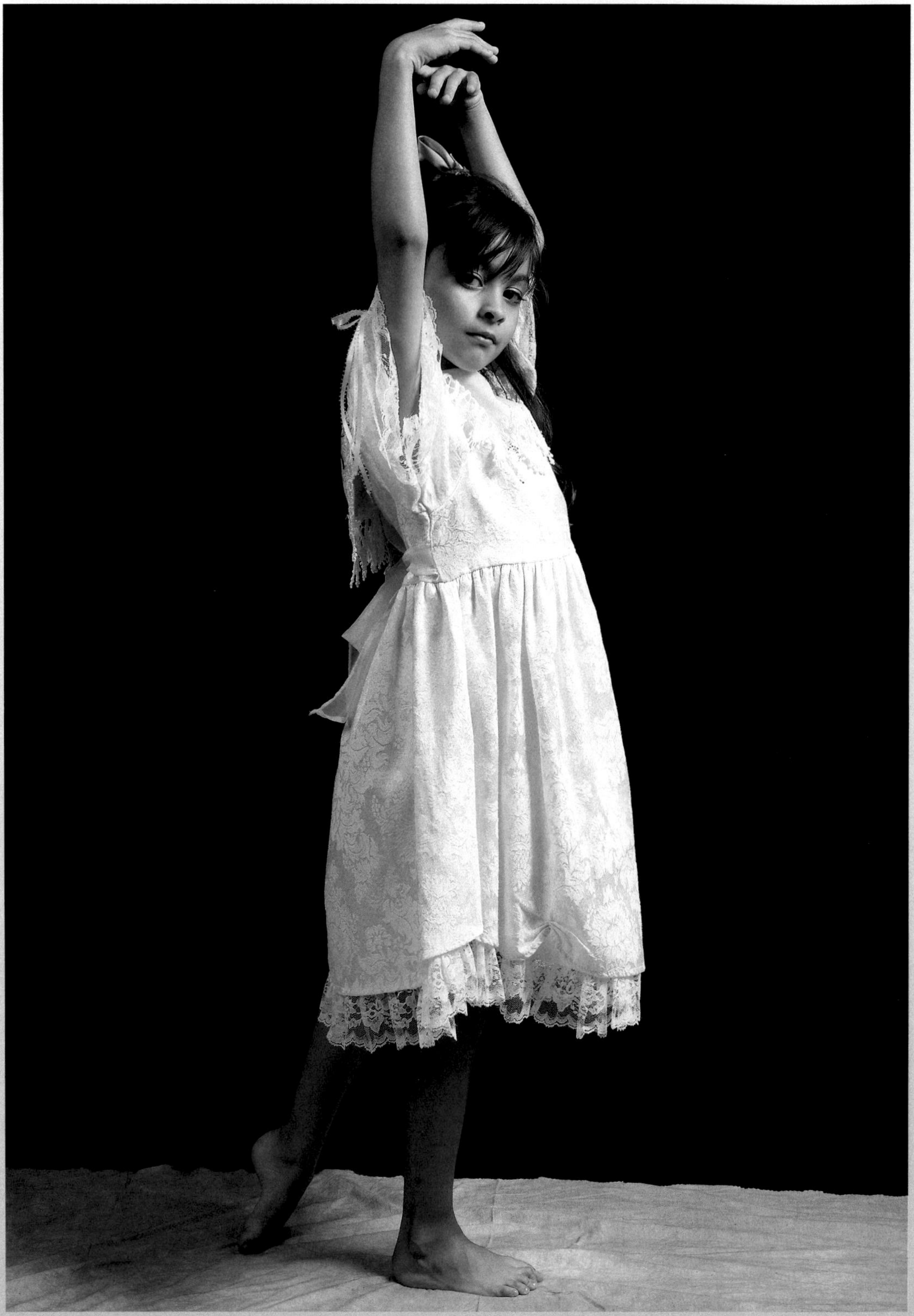

Another ballet pose

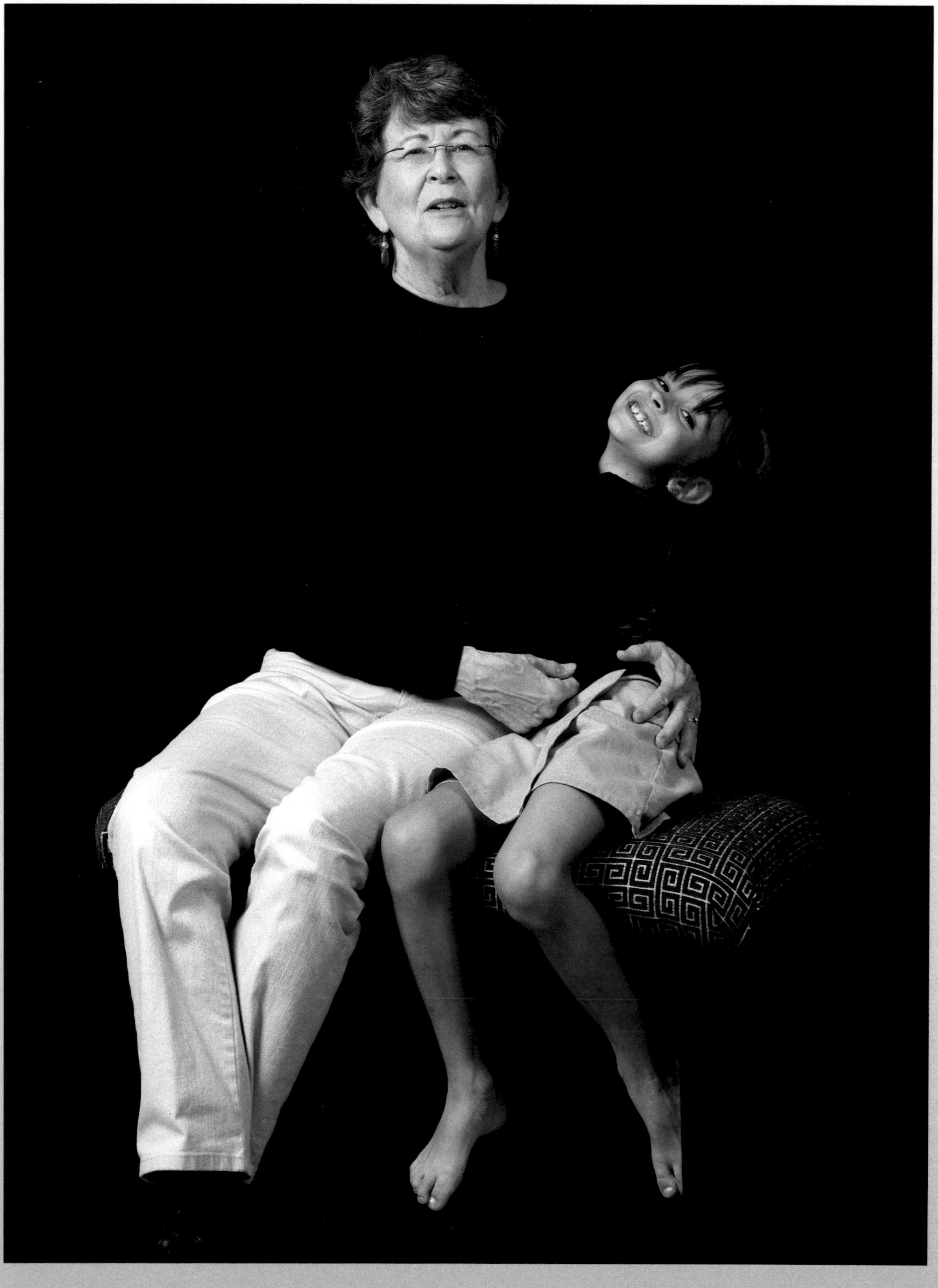

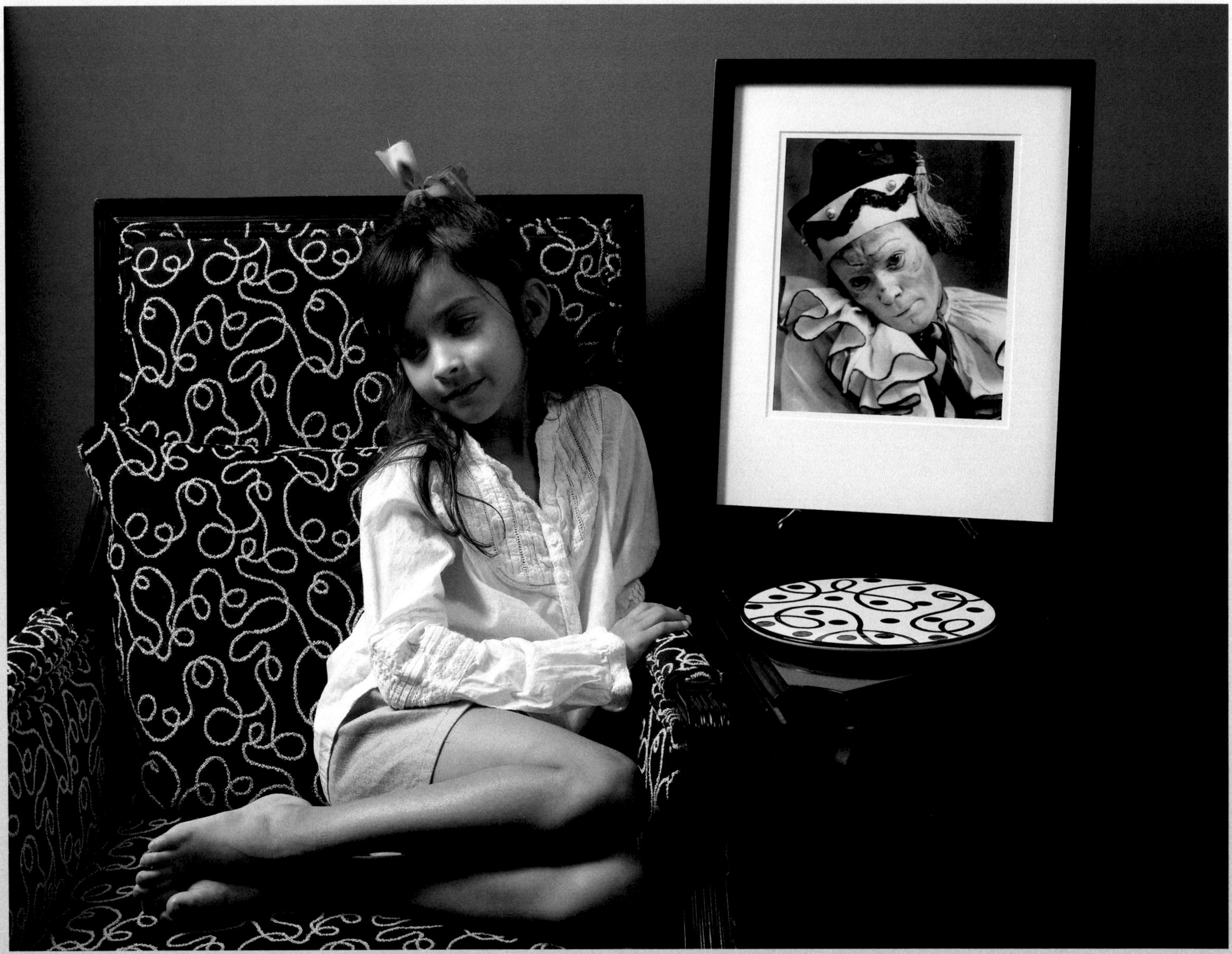

Two dancers

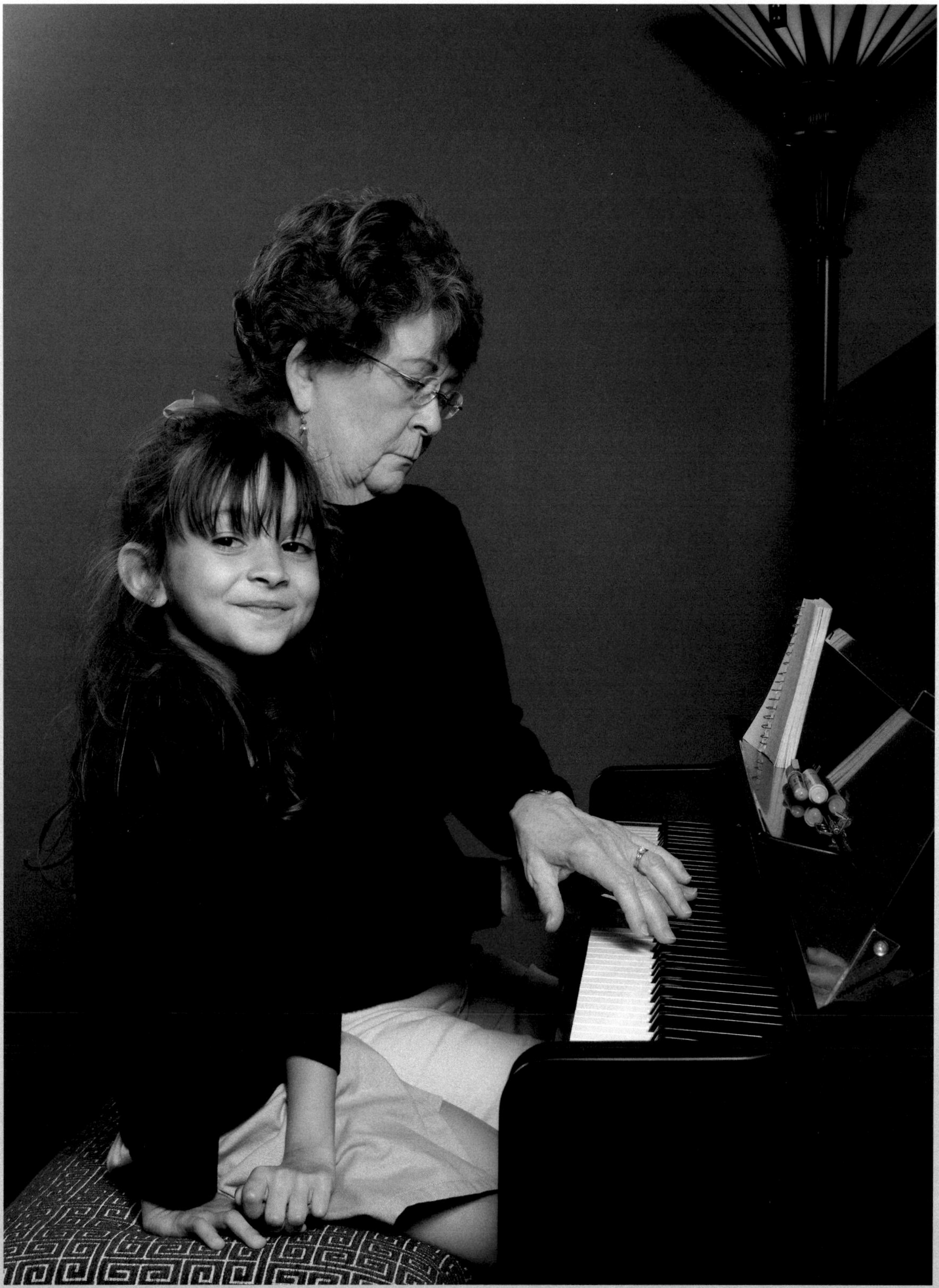

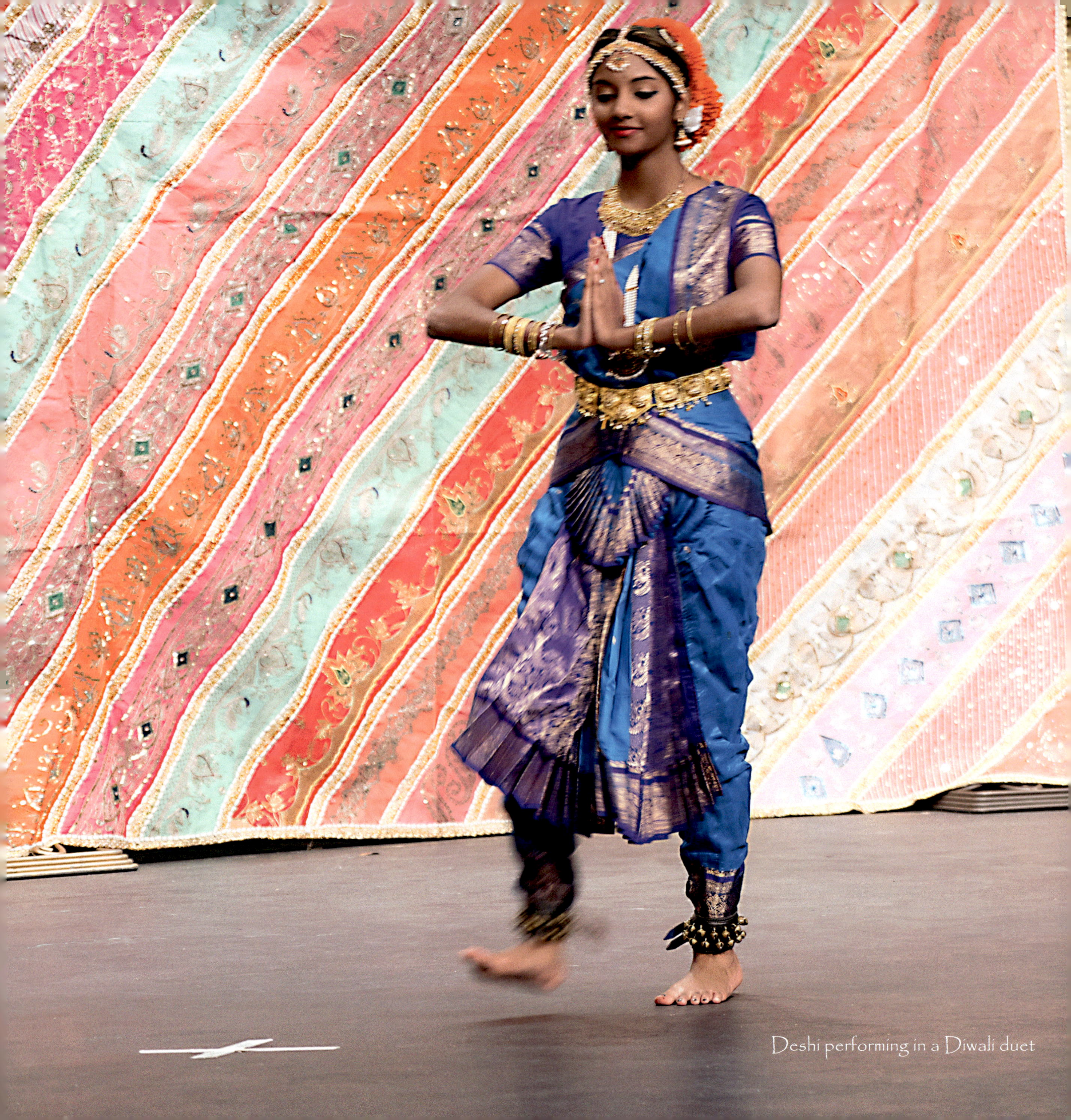

Deshi performing in a Diwali duet

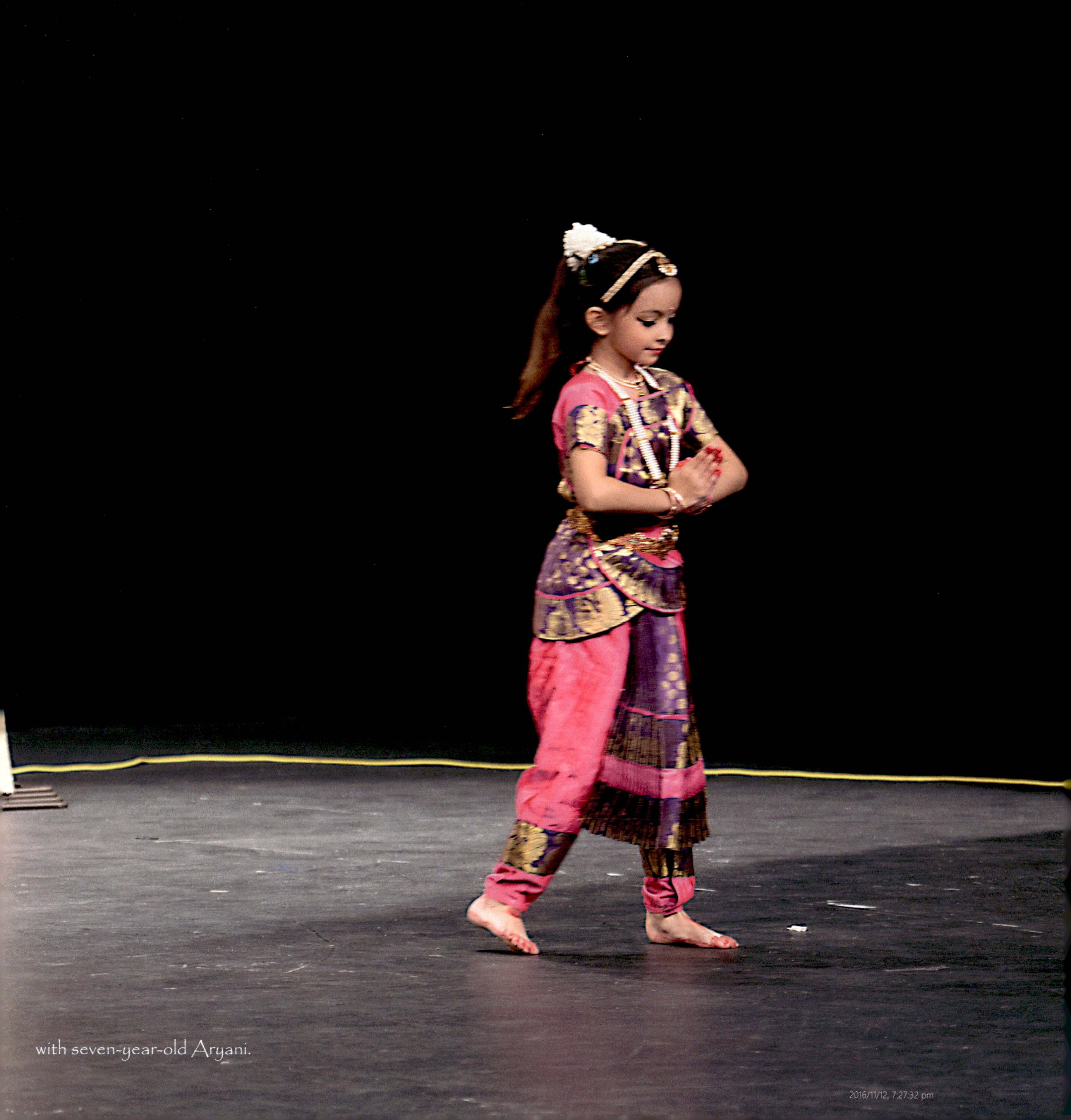


with seven-year-old Aryani.

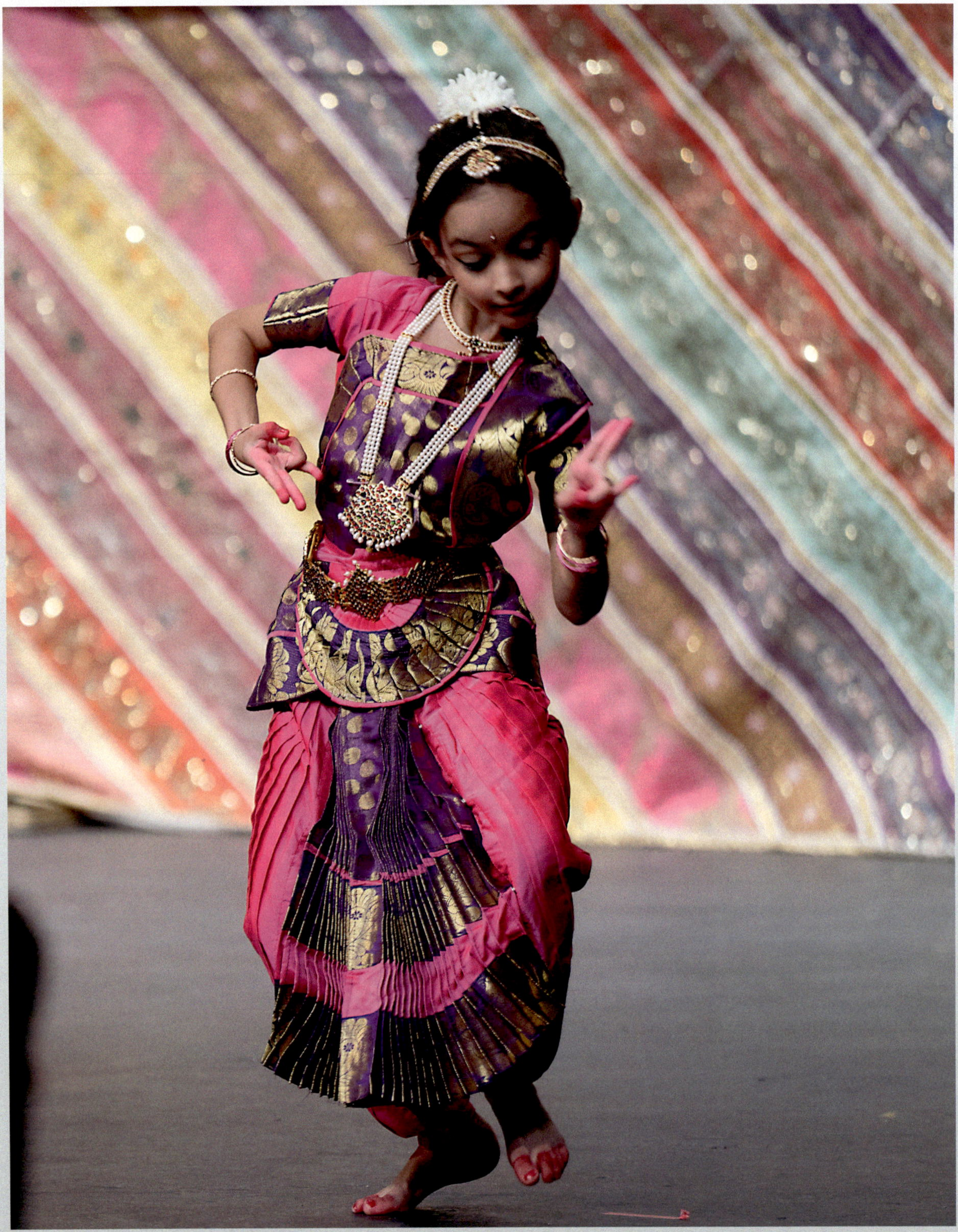

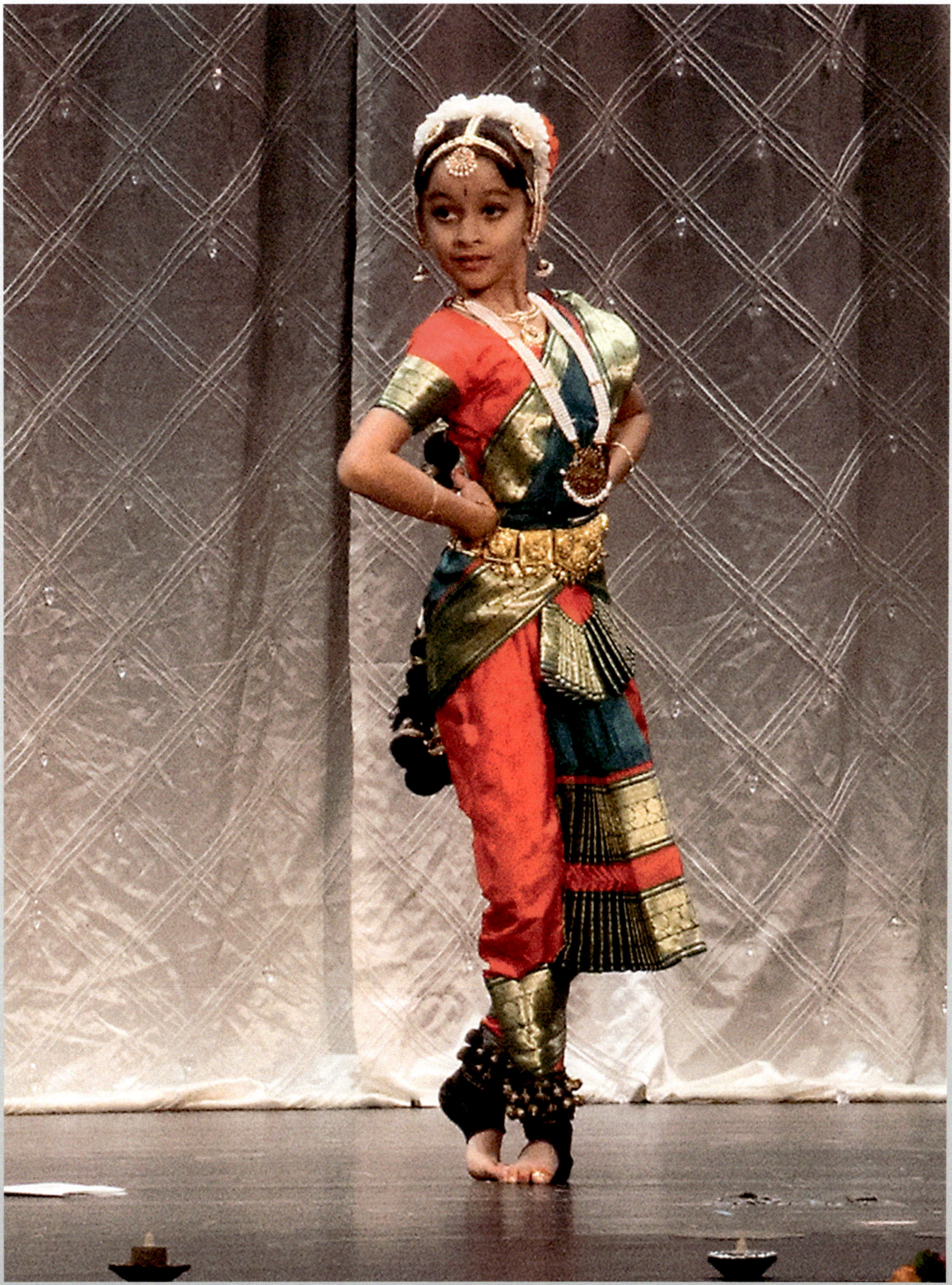

Eight-year-old Aryani in a Diwali solo

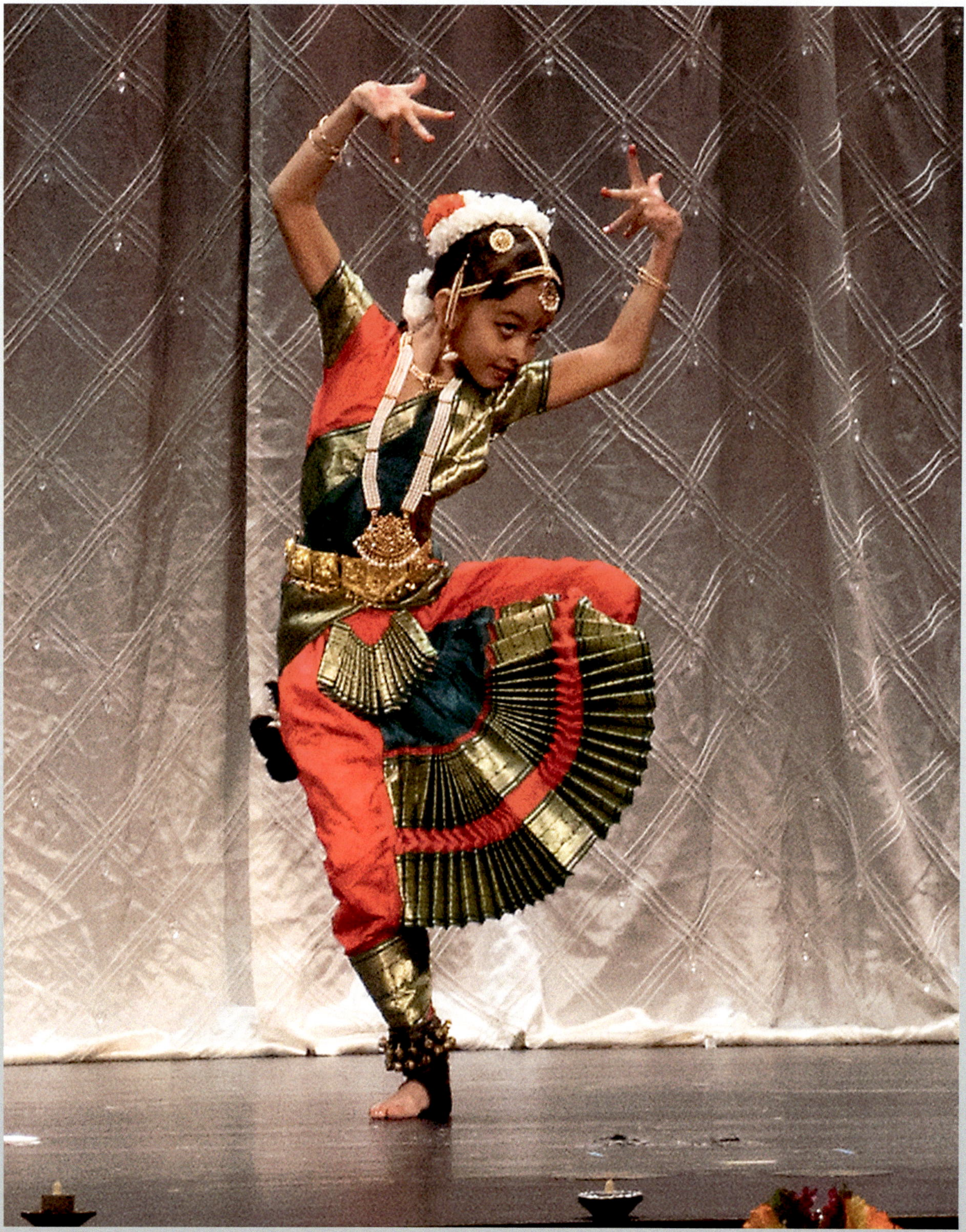

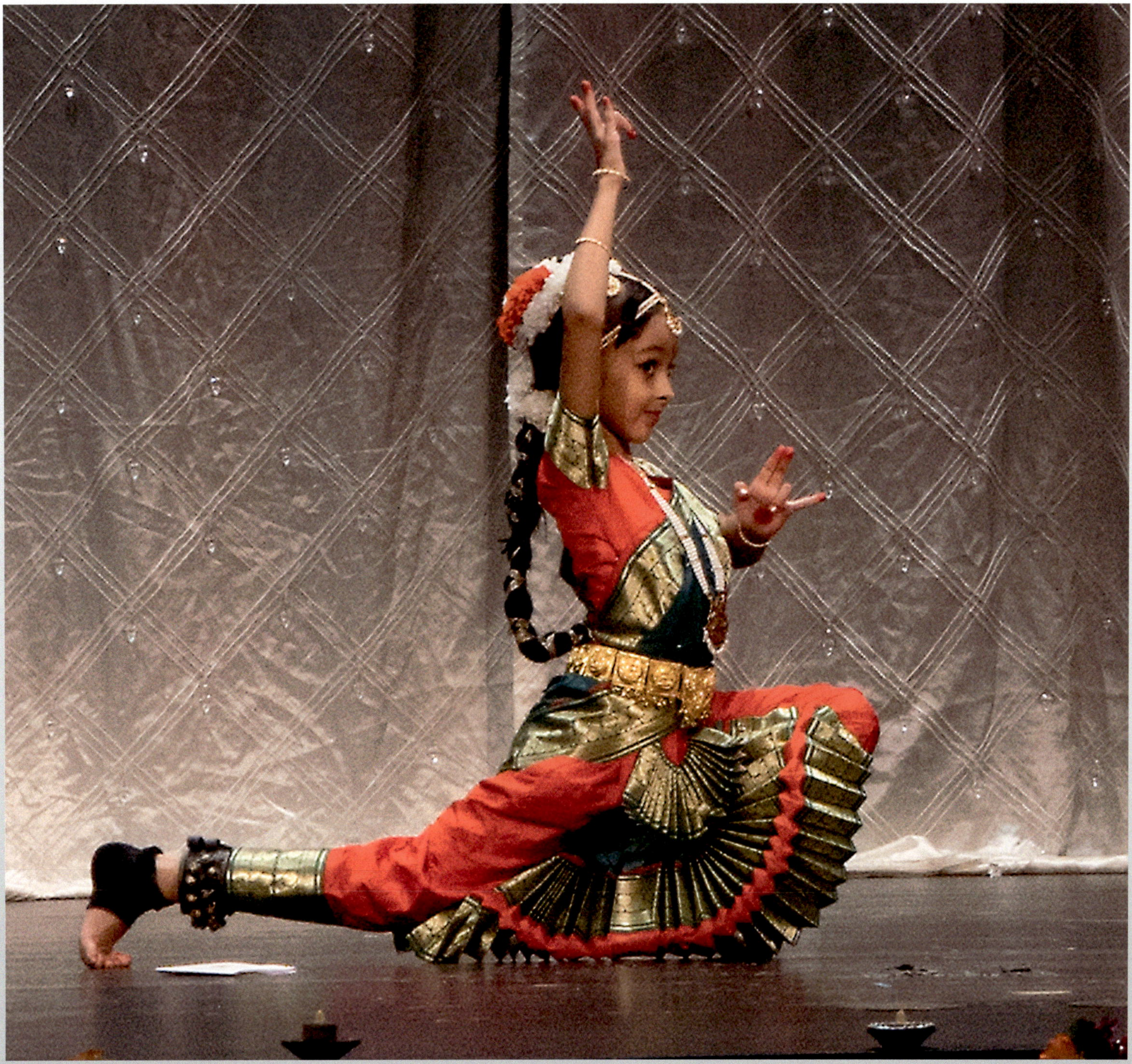

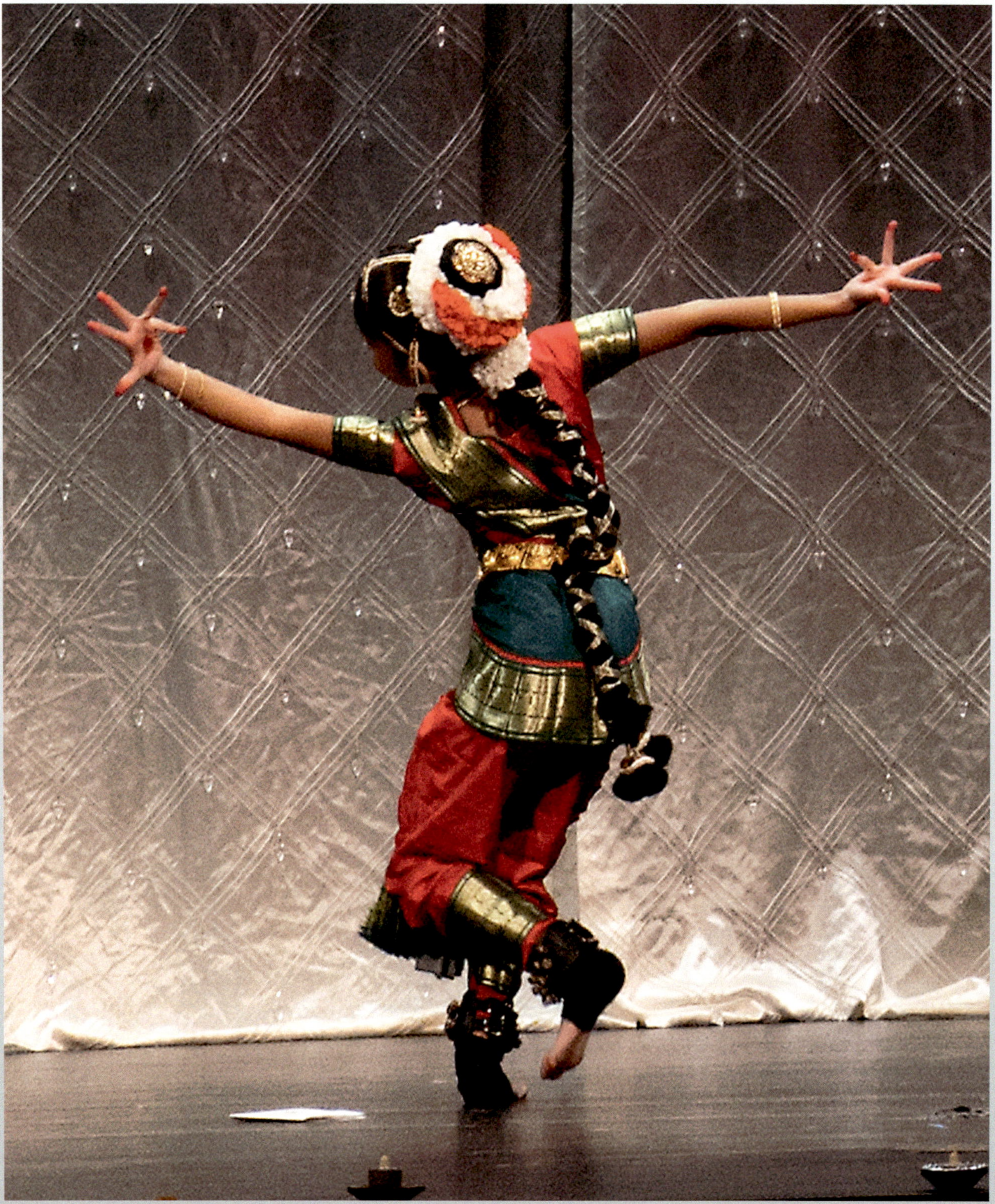



2017/10/21, 7:14:20 pm

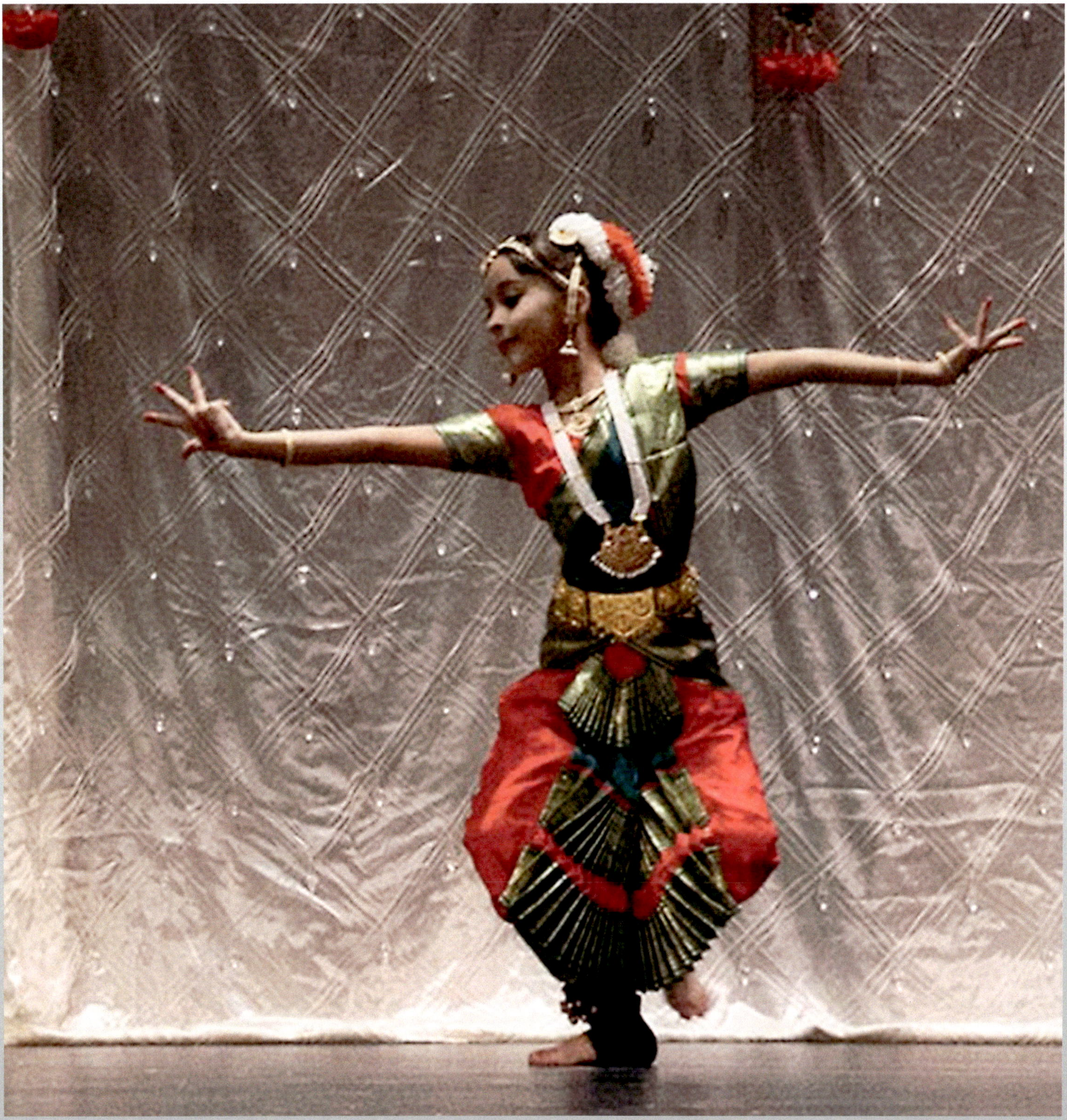

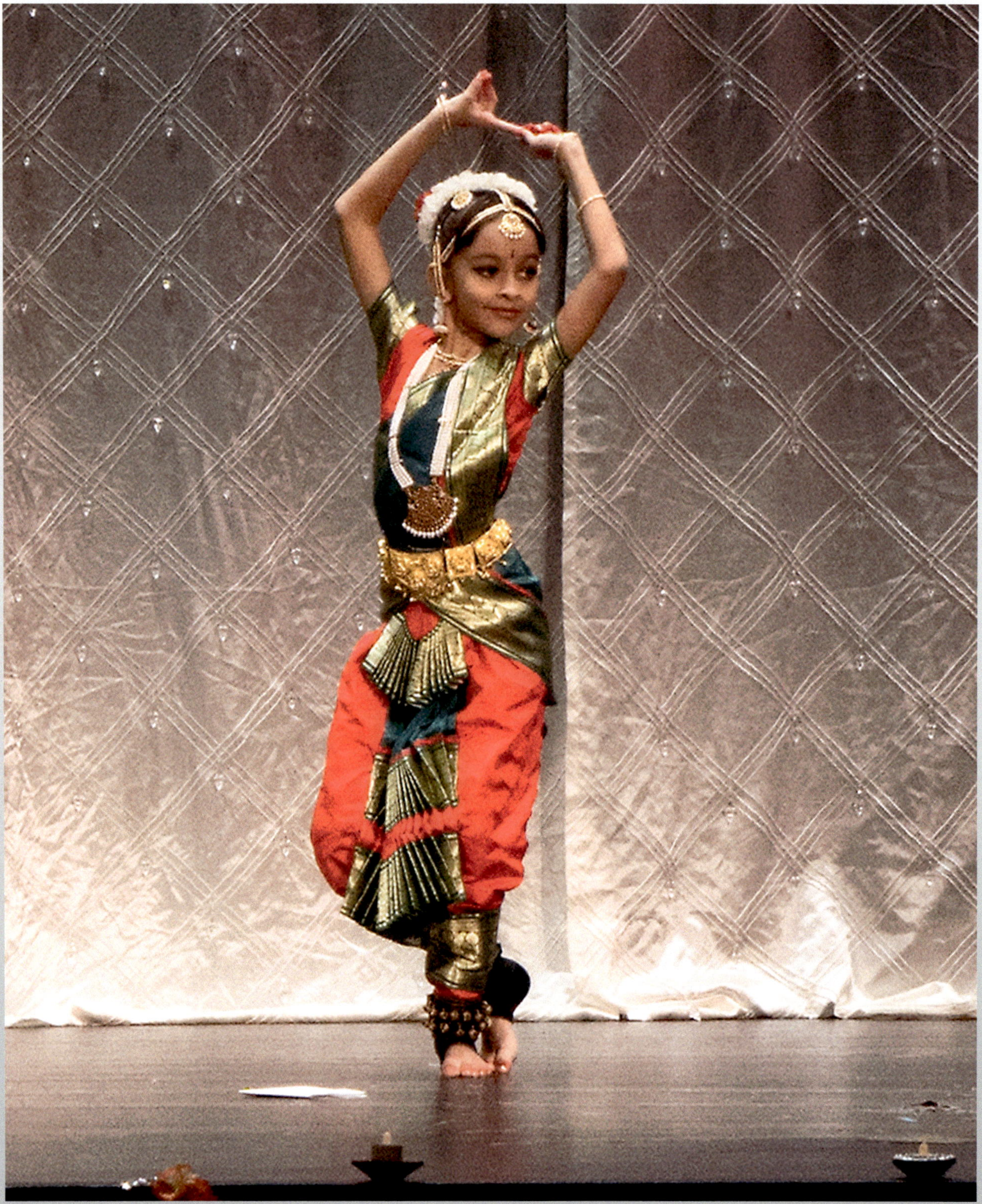



2017/10/21, 7:11:20 pm

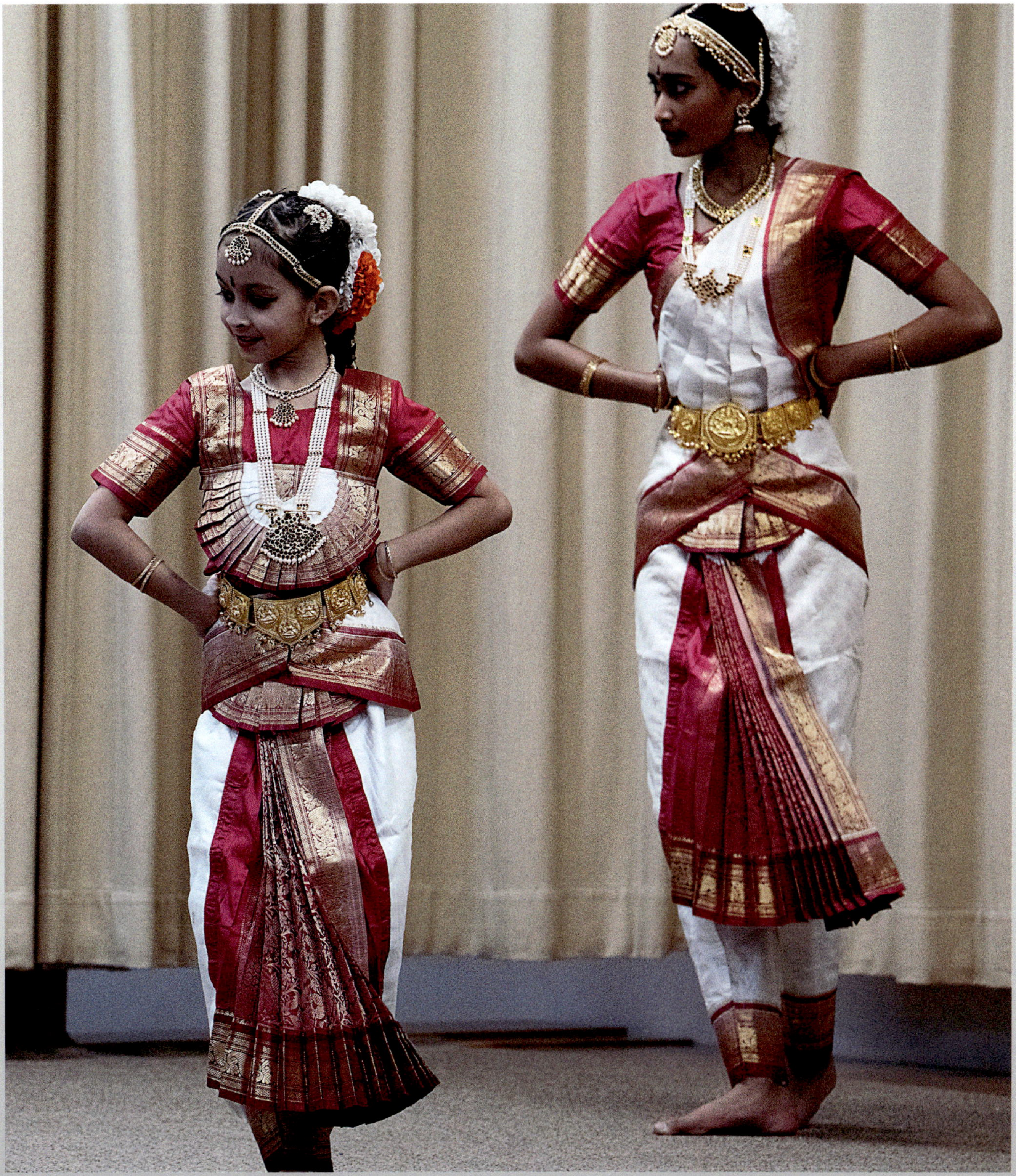

Ponga New Year Festival at age eight

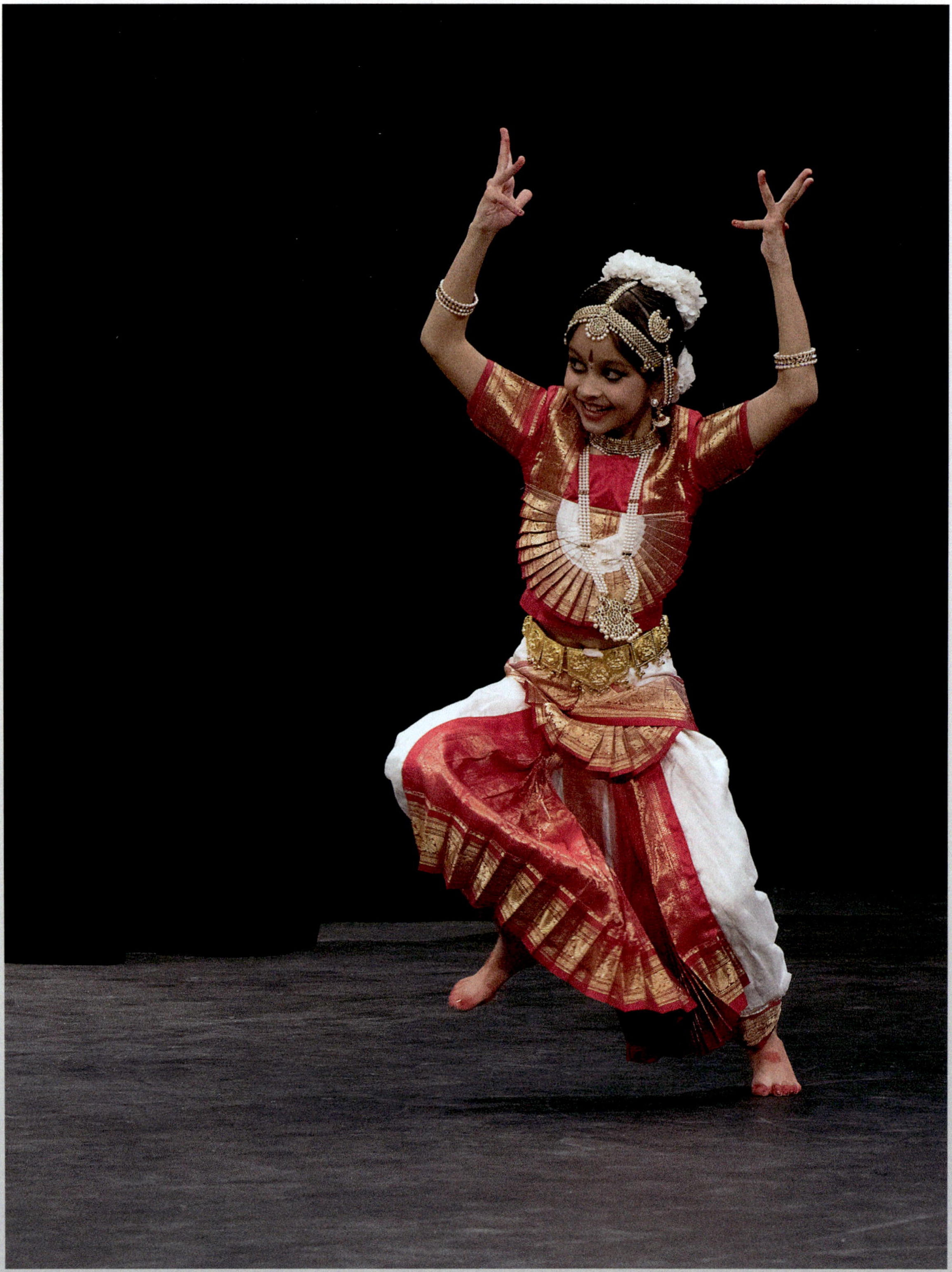

Holi 2018 clebration solo at age eight

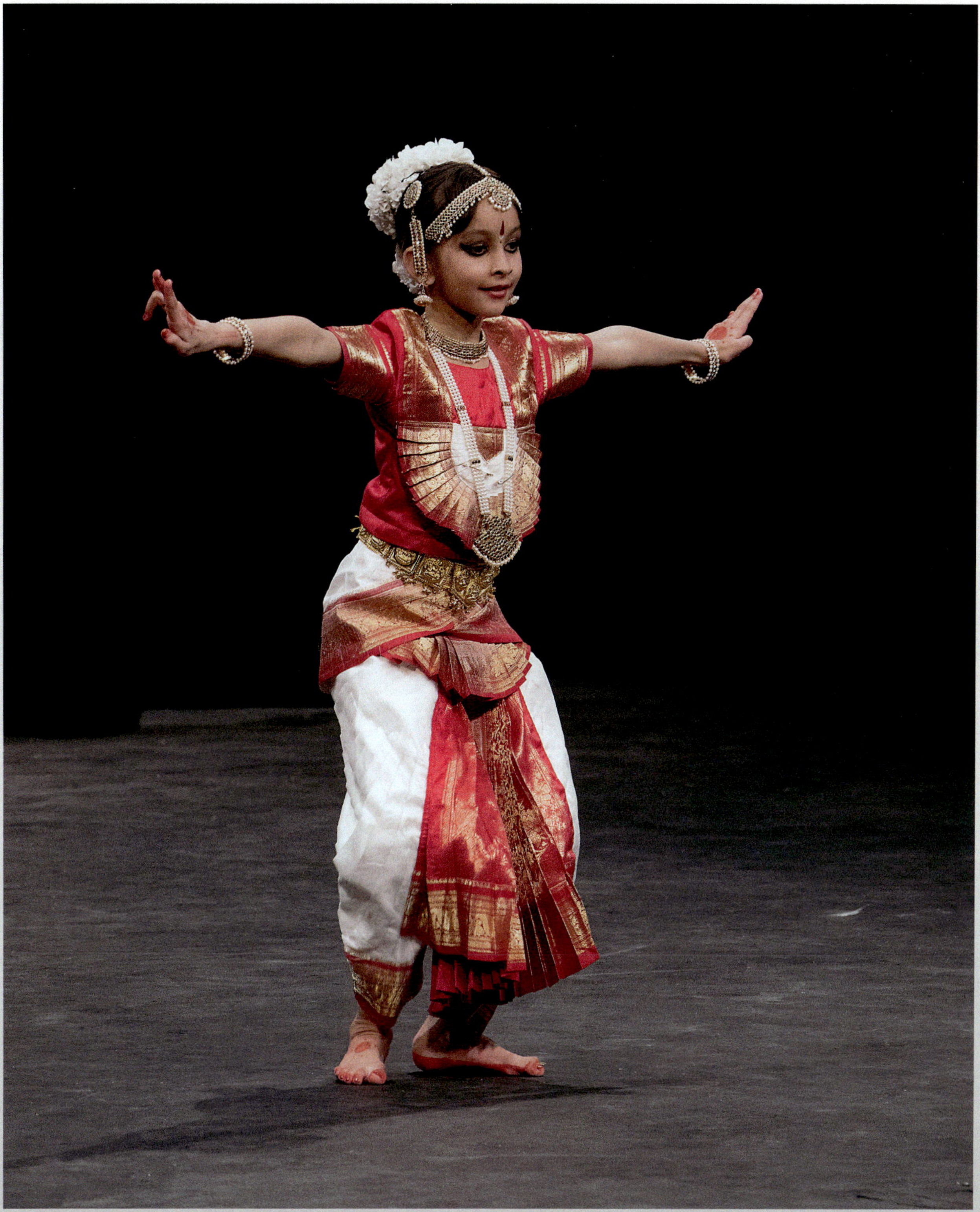

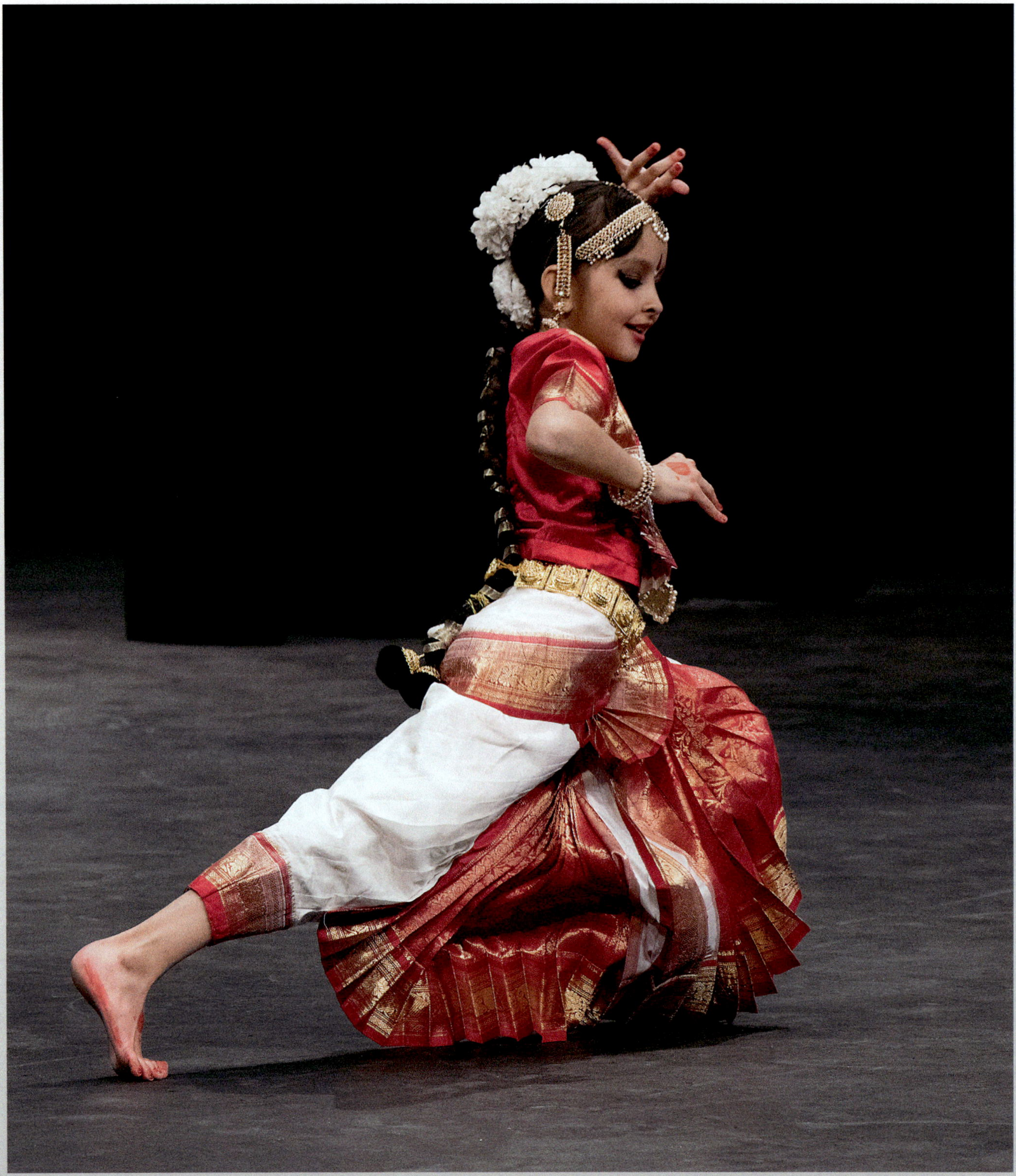


2018/03/24, 8:48:24 pm

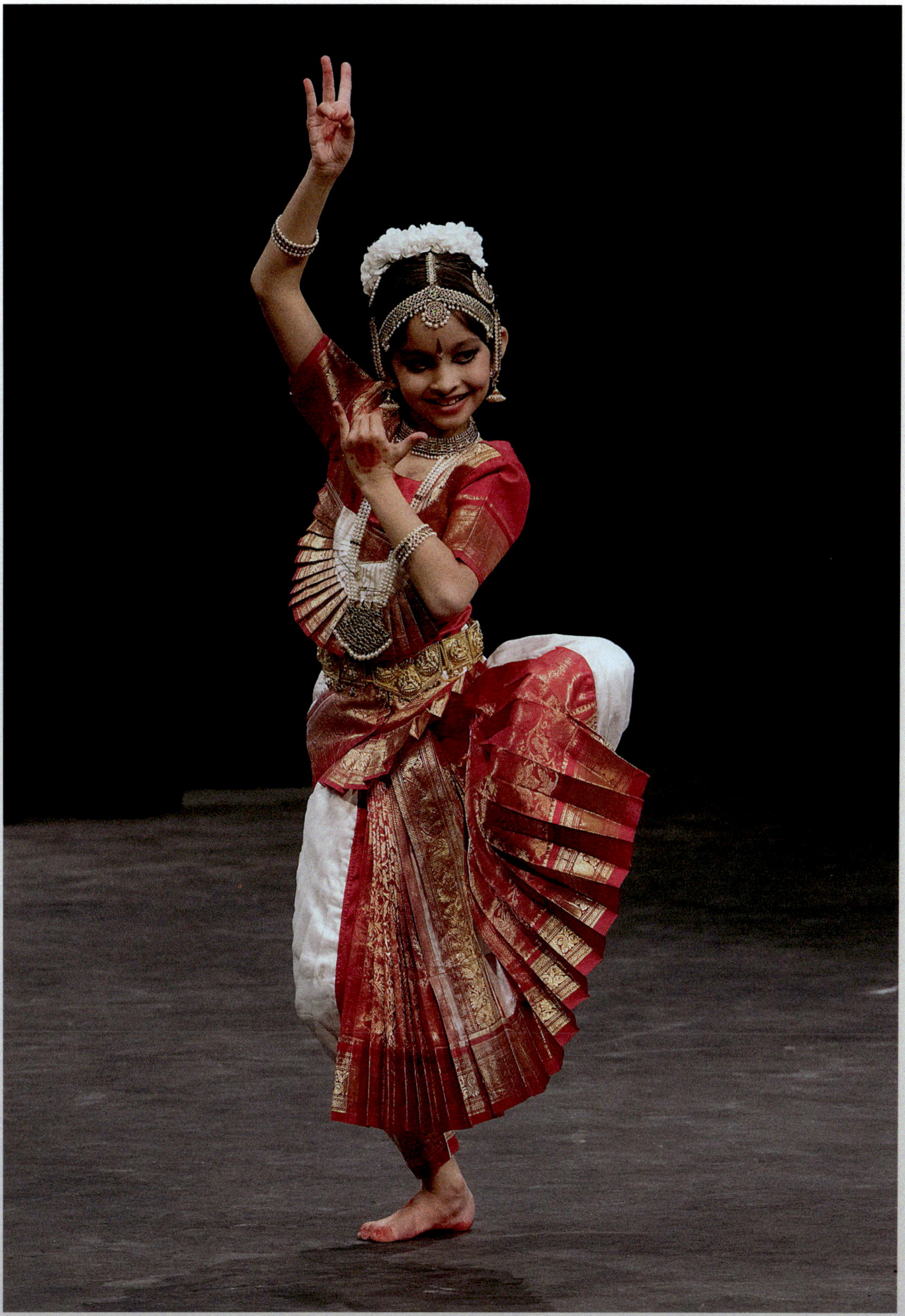

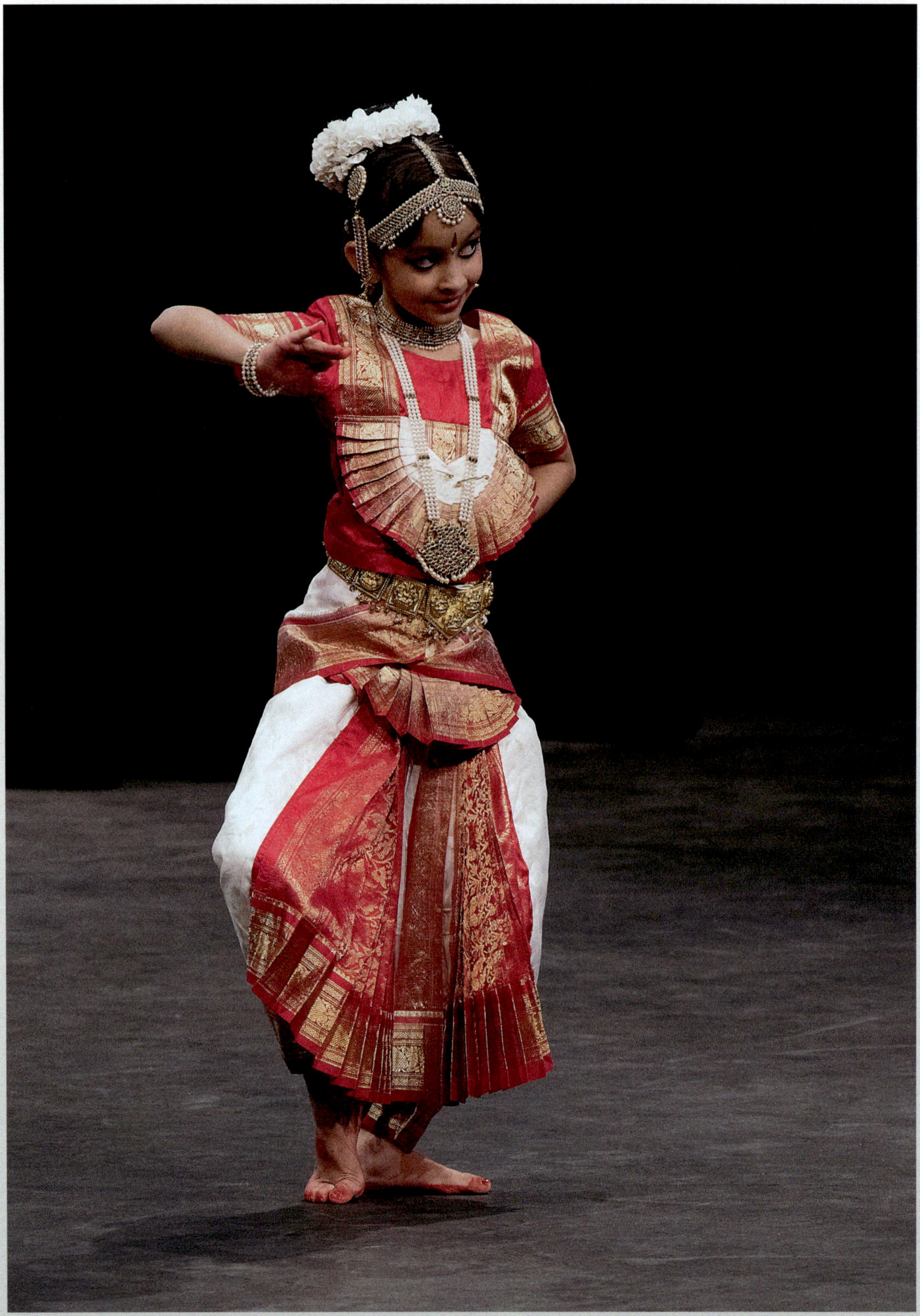


2018/03/24, 8:47:22 pm

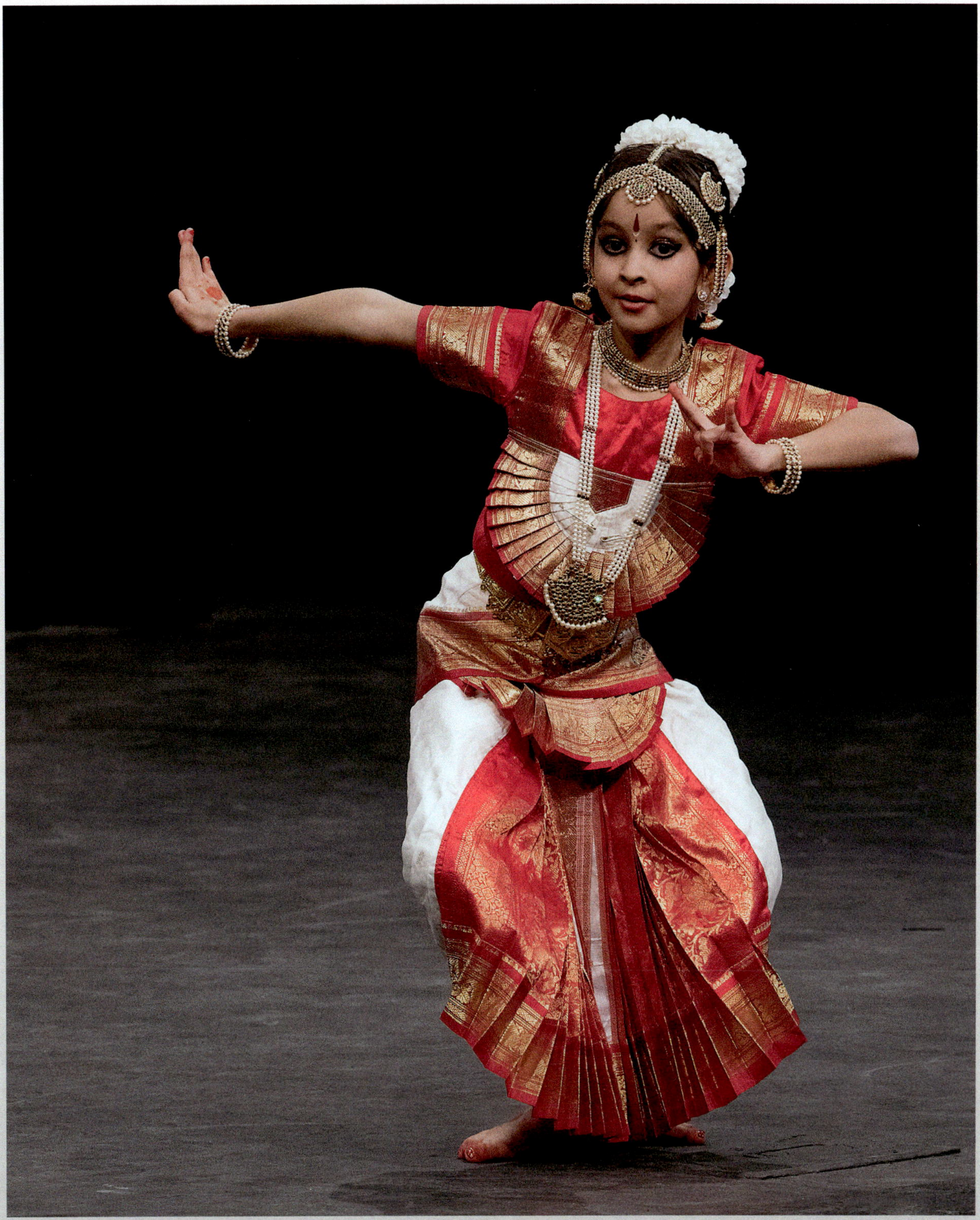

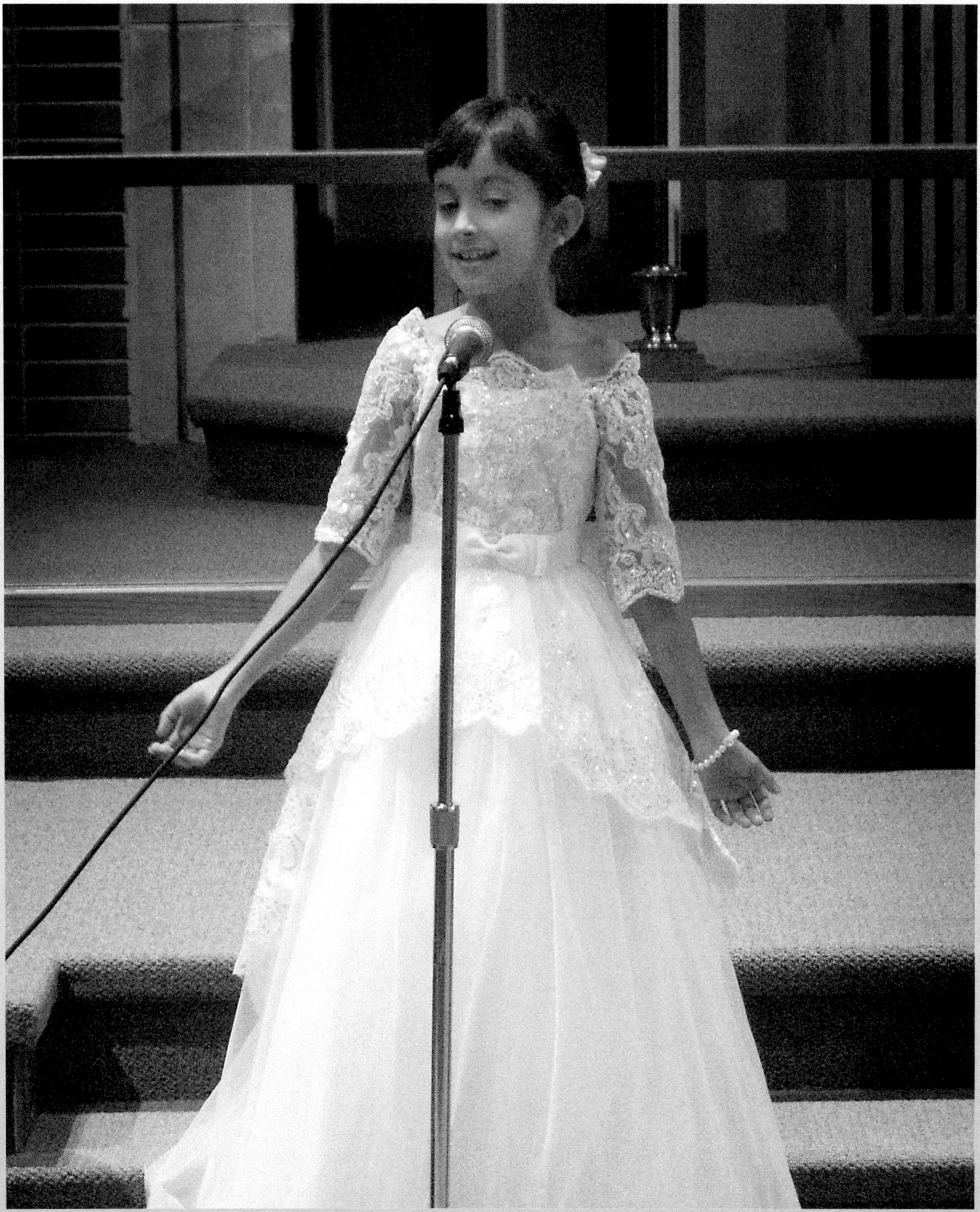

Voice recital at age eight

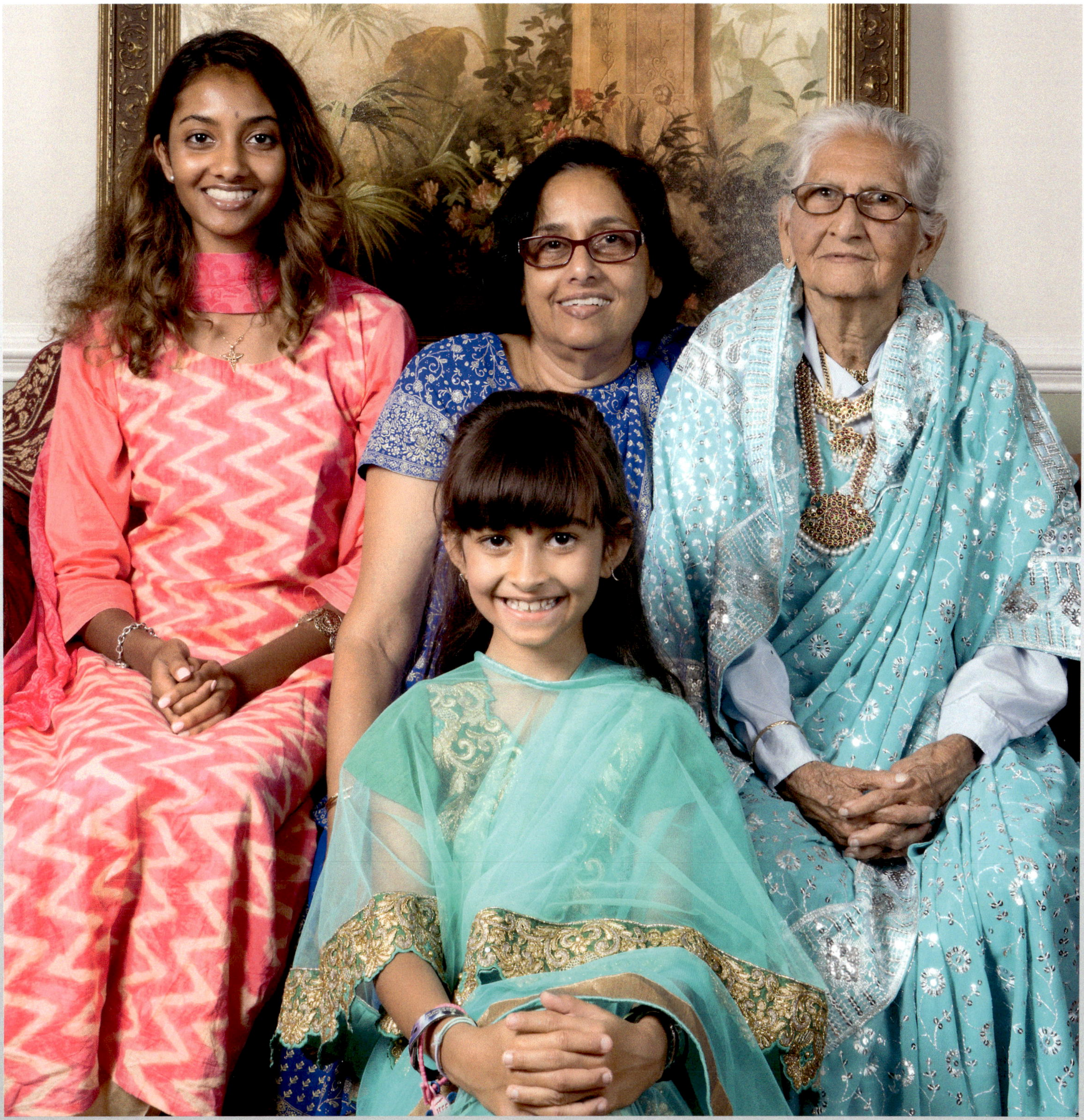

Aryani at nine years old, amidst four generations

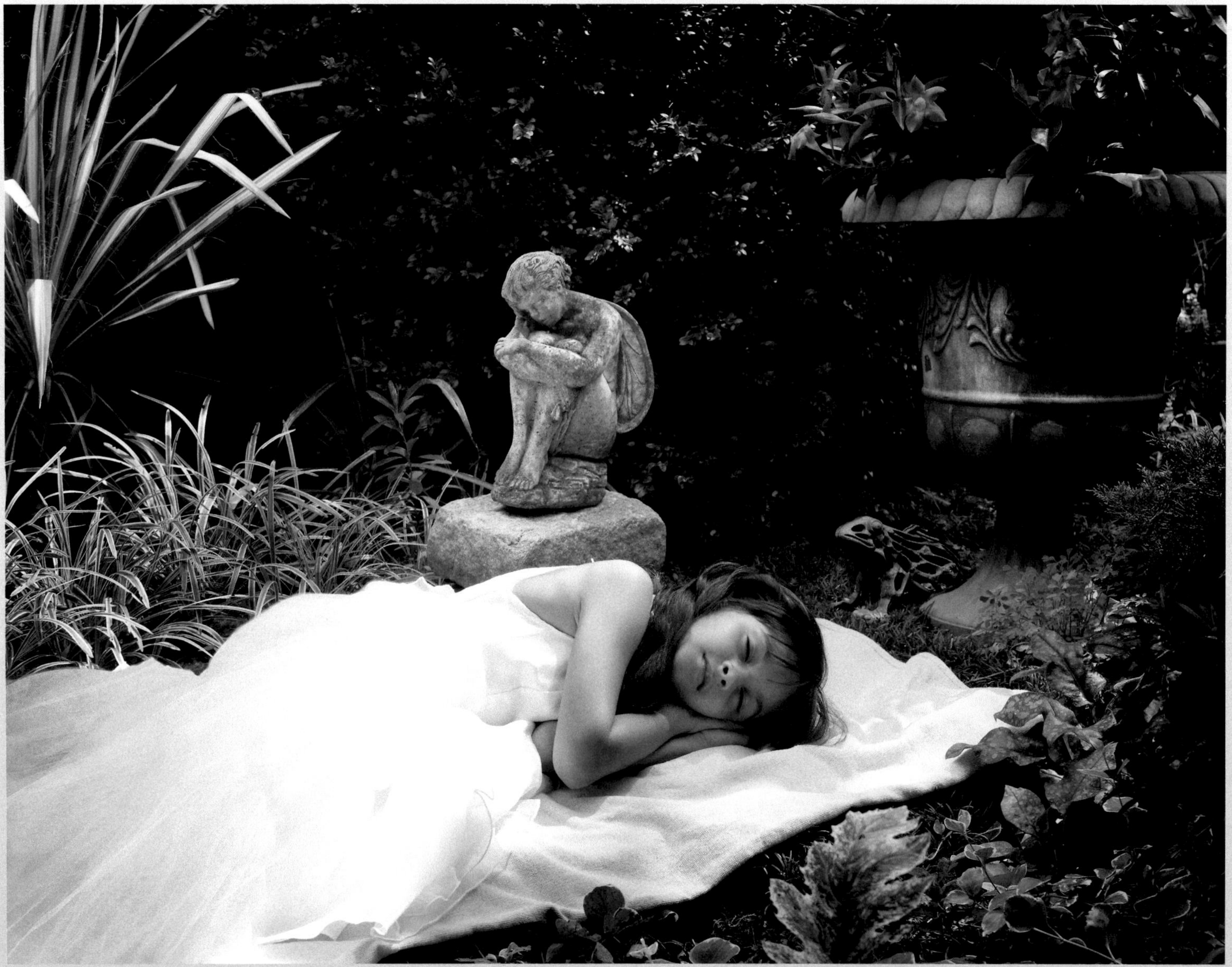

Aryani in Jack's Garden, age nine

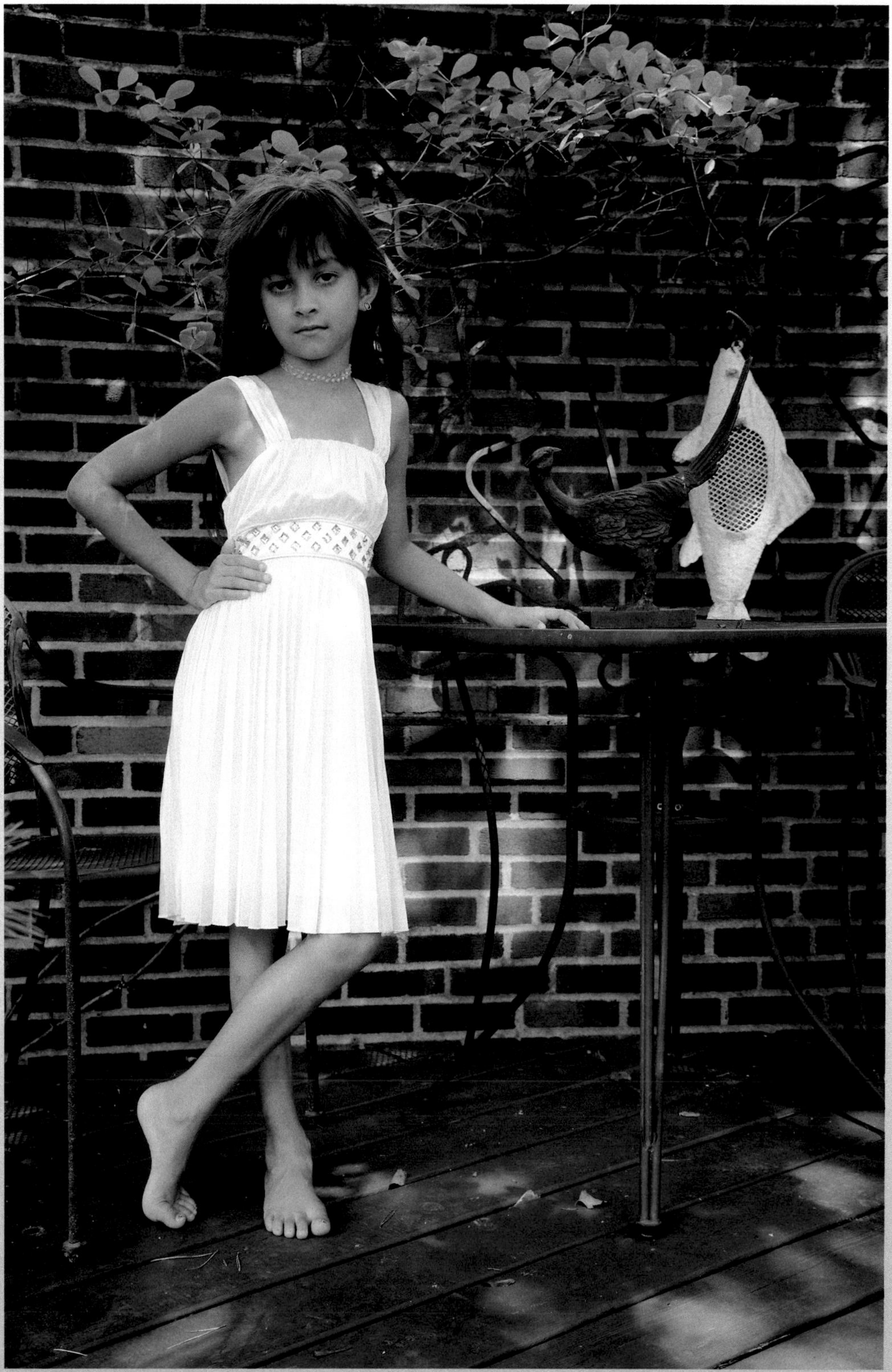

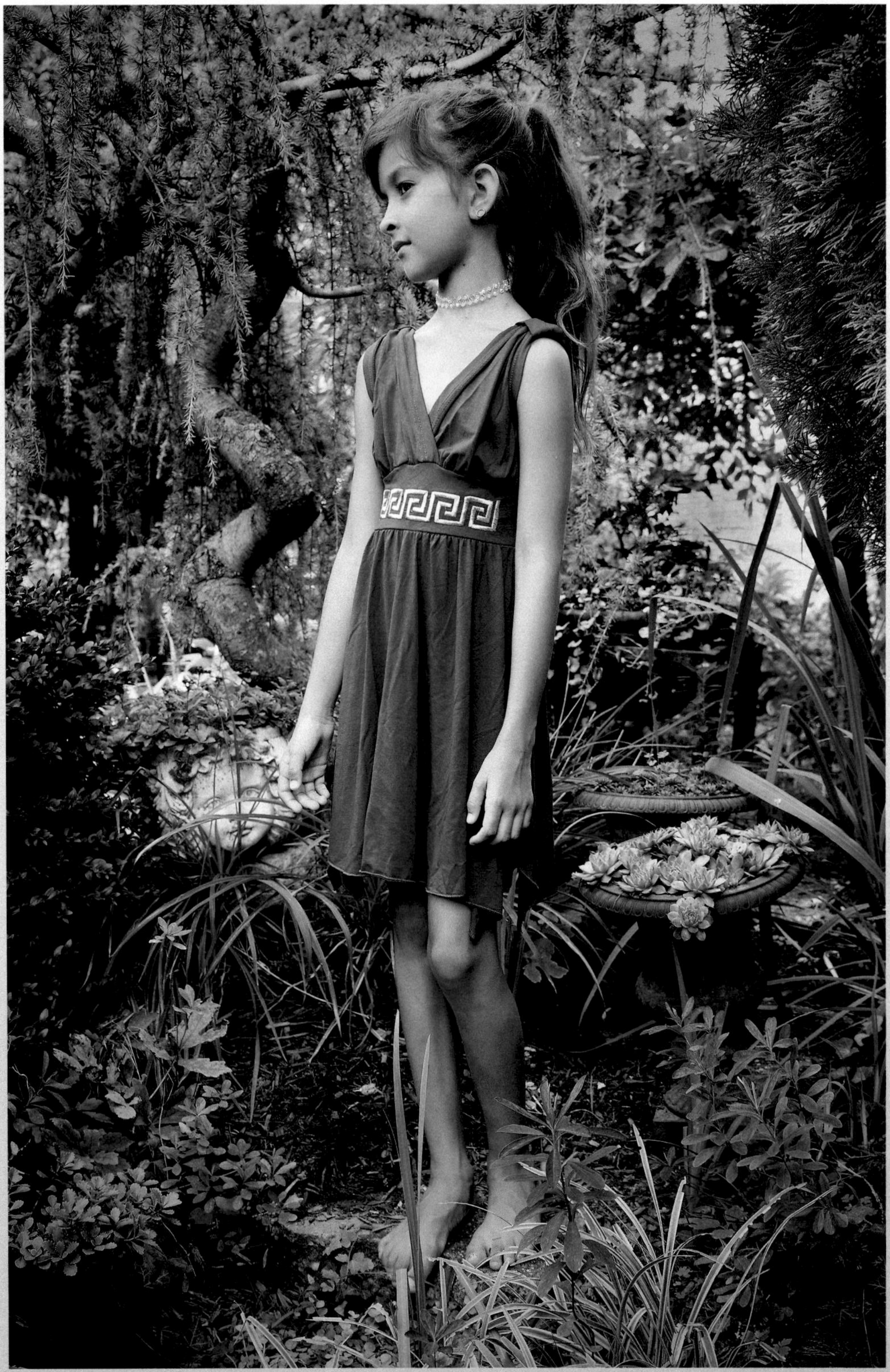

Wood nymph

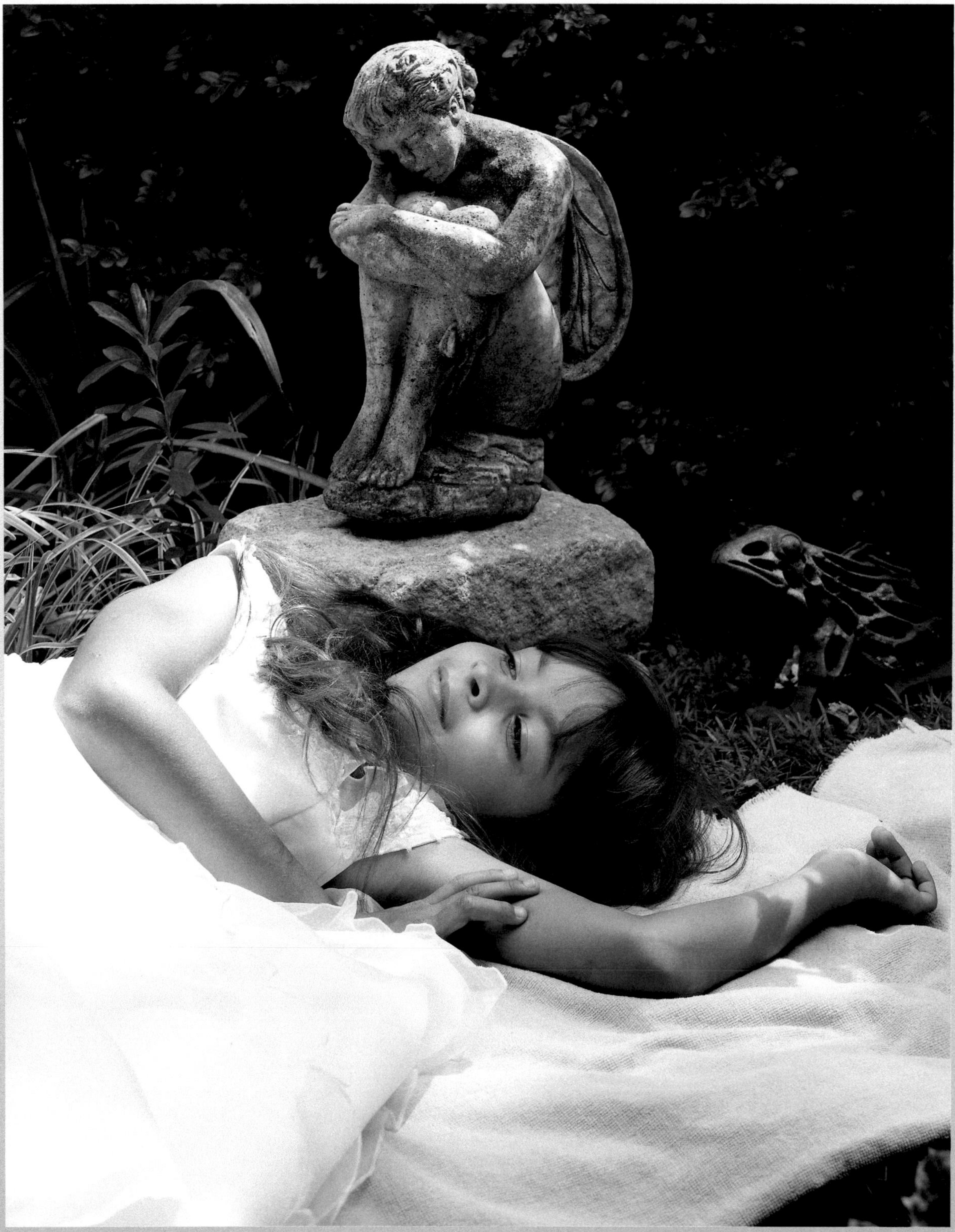

Waking dream

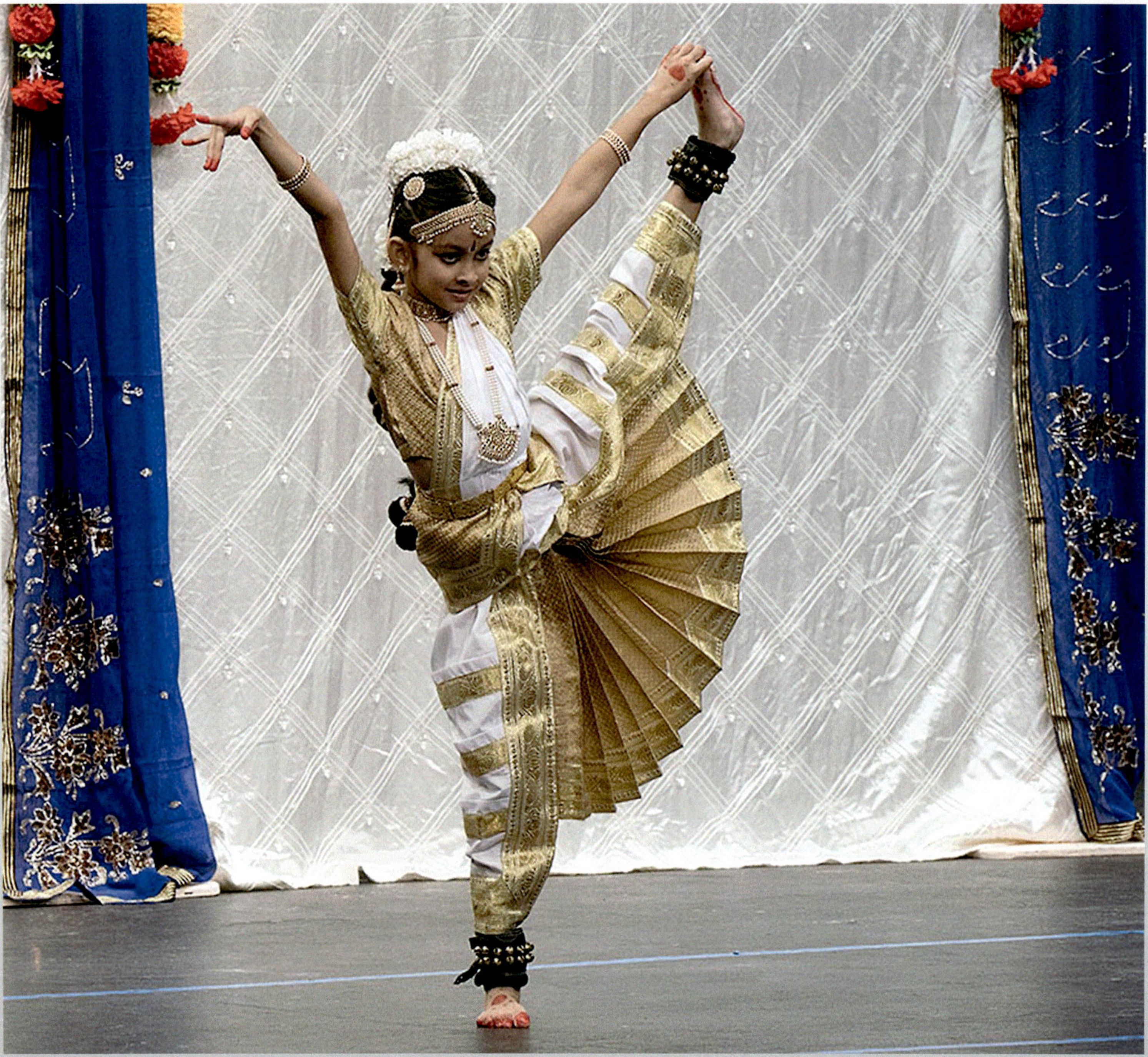

Diwali celebration solo at nine years old

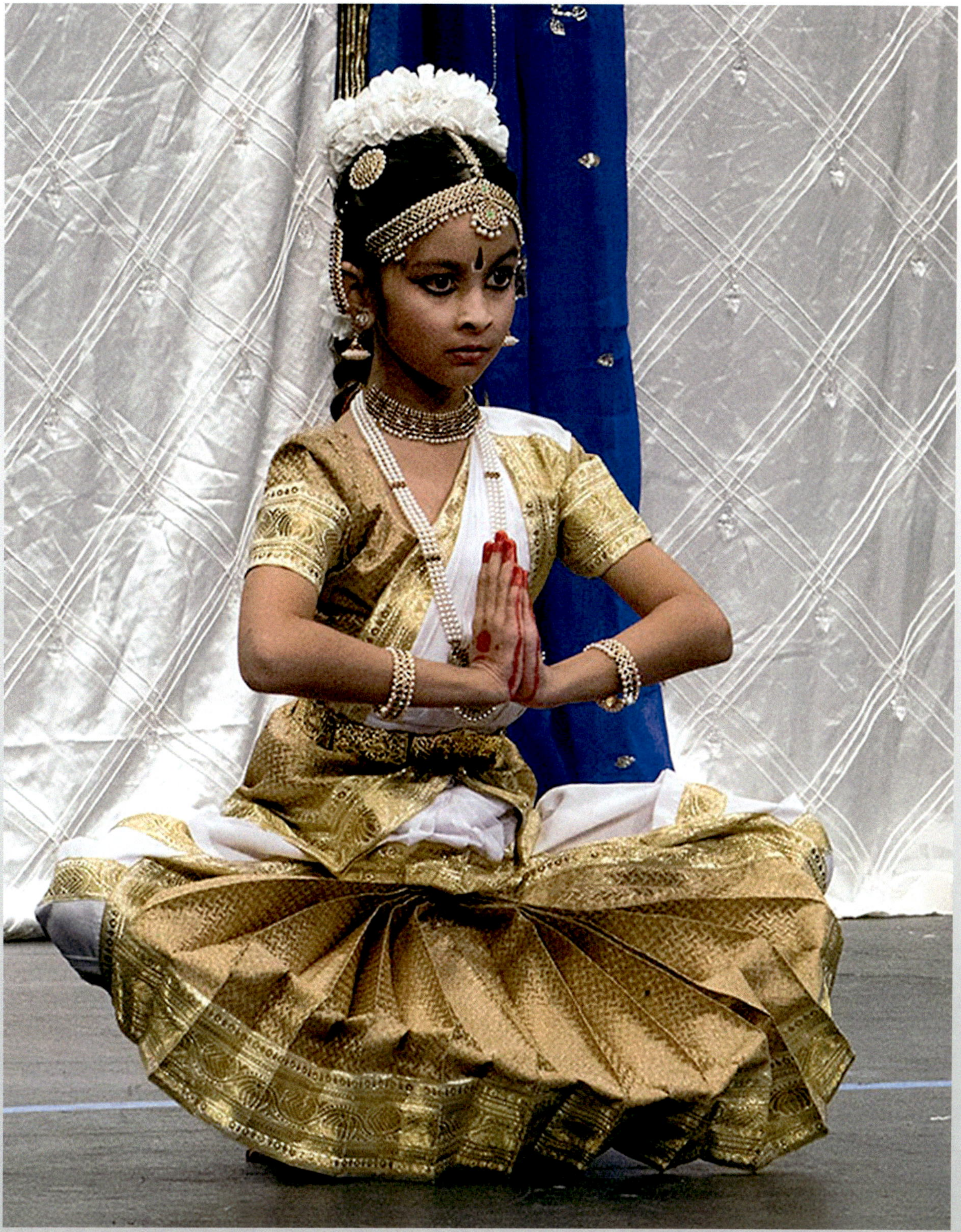

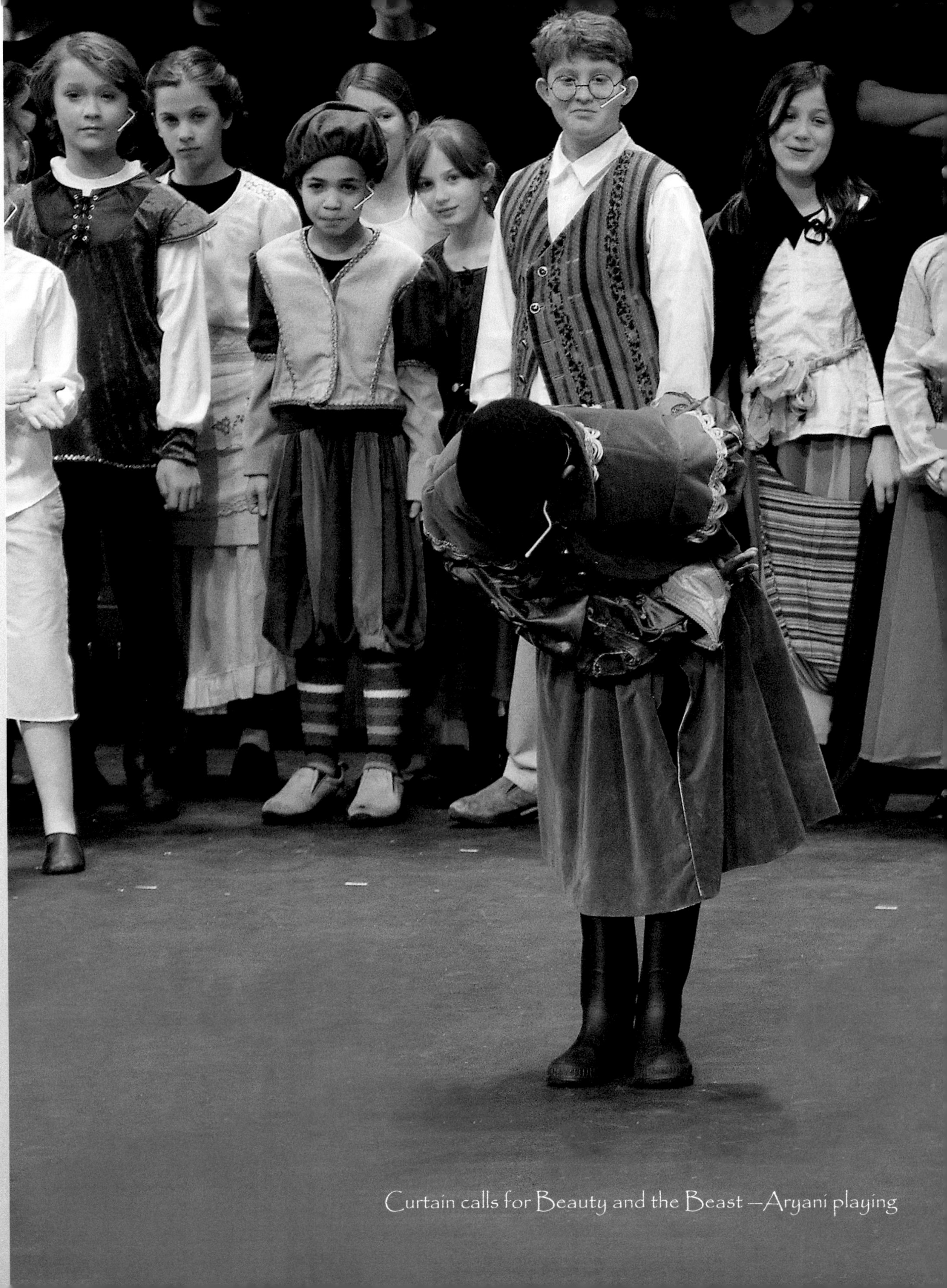

Curtain calls for Beauty and the Beast —Aryani playing

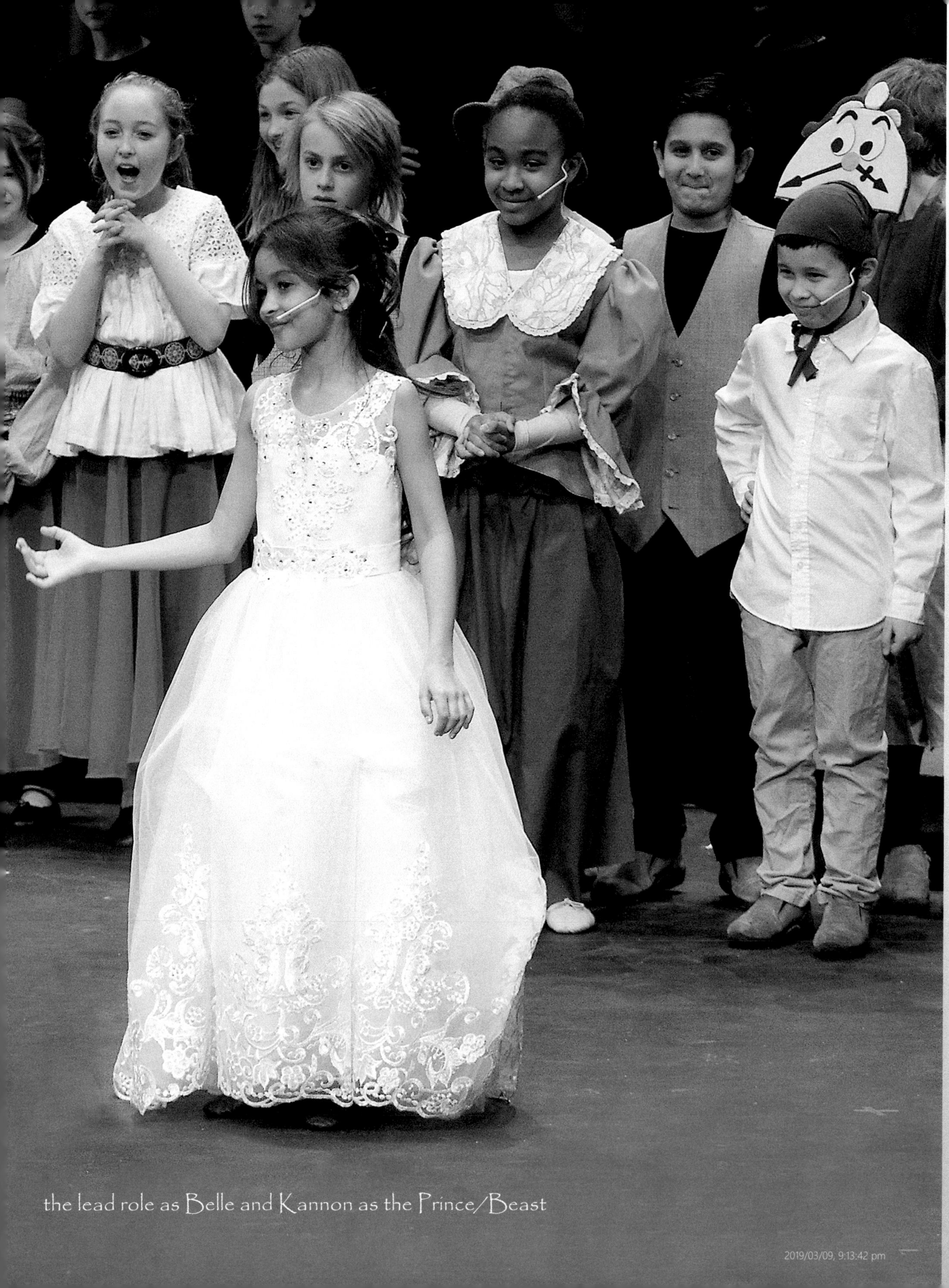


the lead role as Belle and Kannon as the Prince/Beast

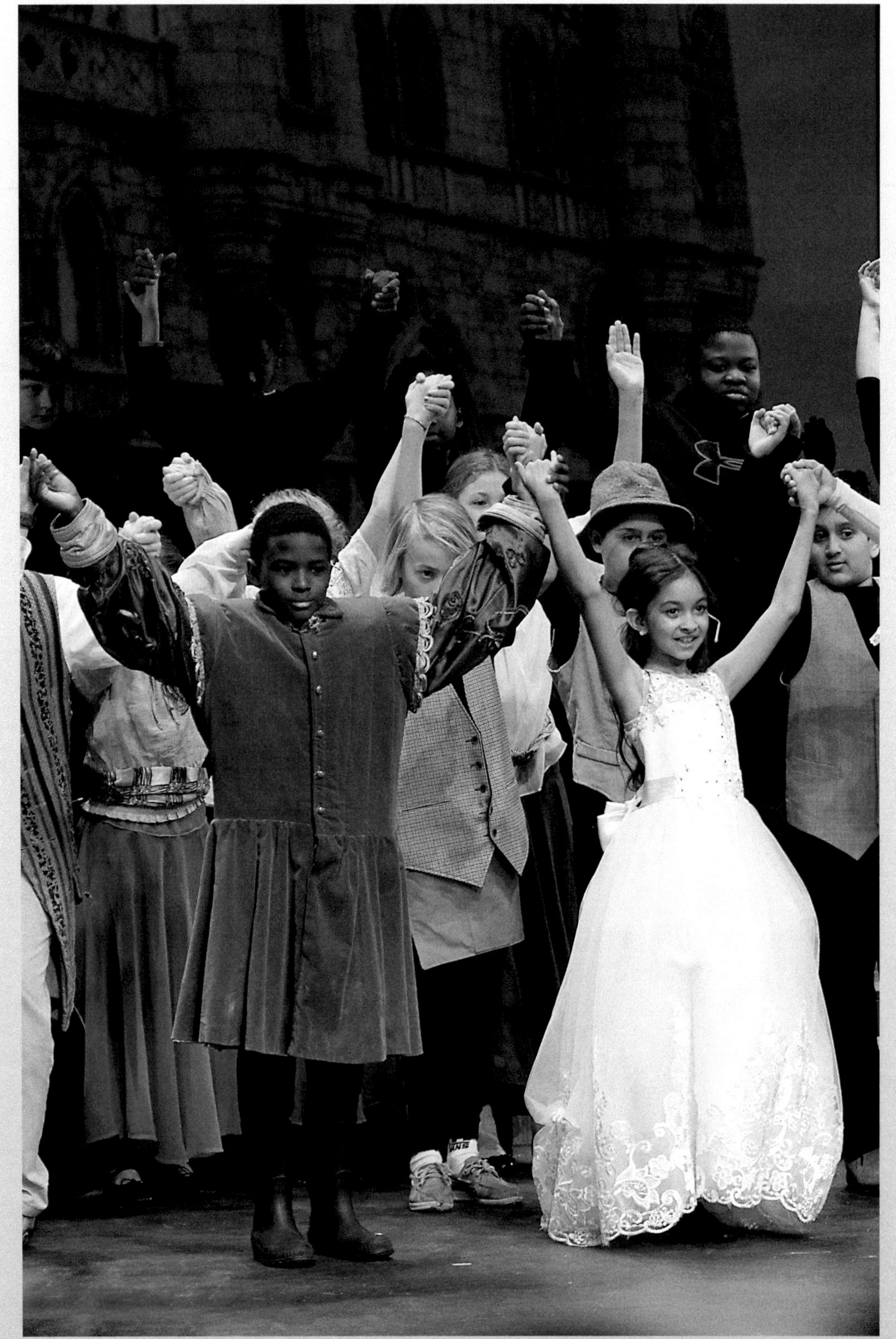



2019/03/10, 2:13:53 pm

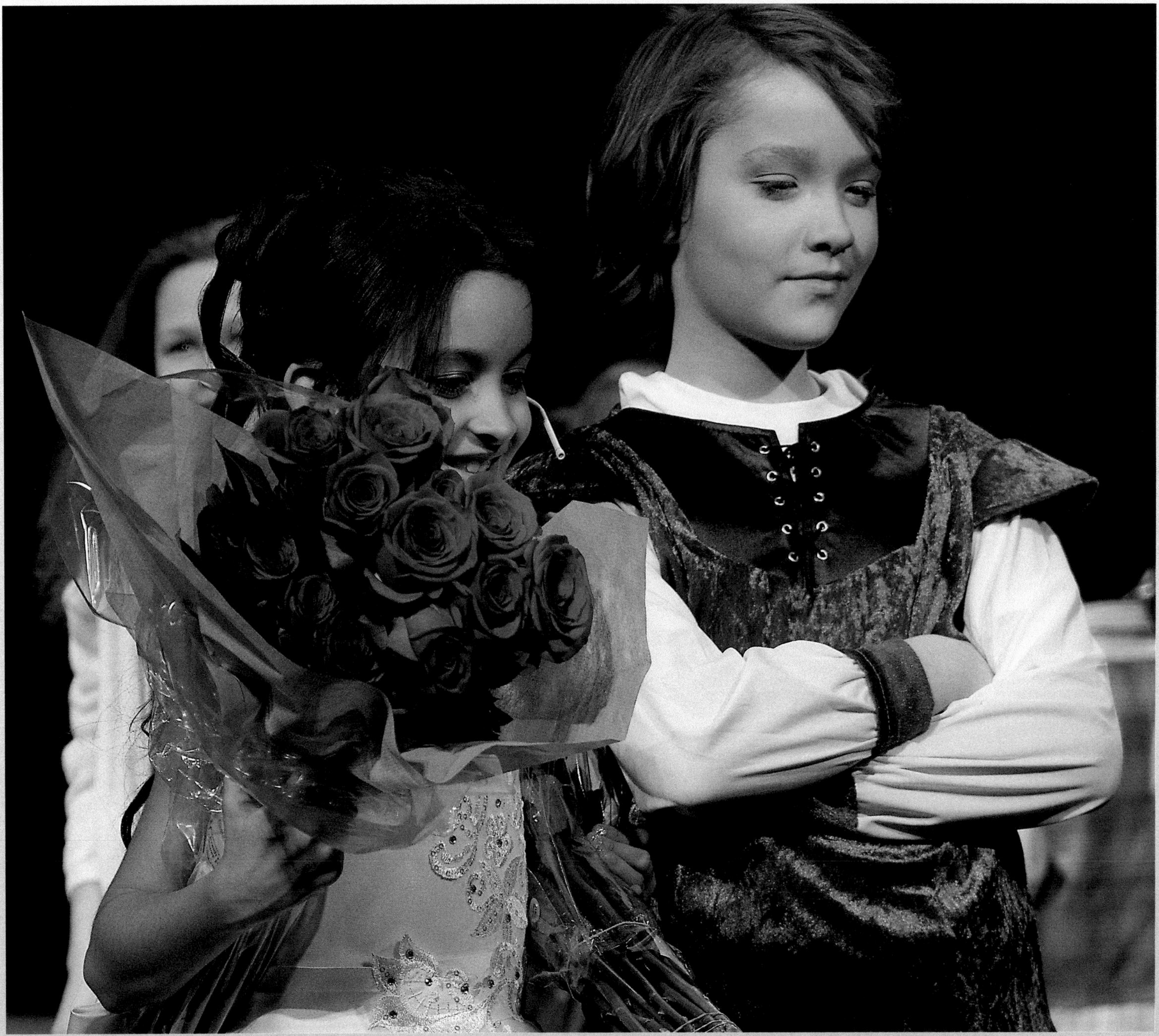

Belle and Gaston (James)

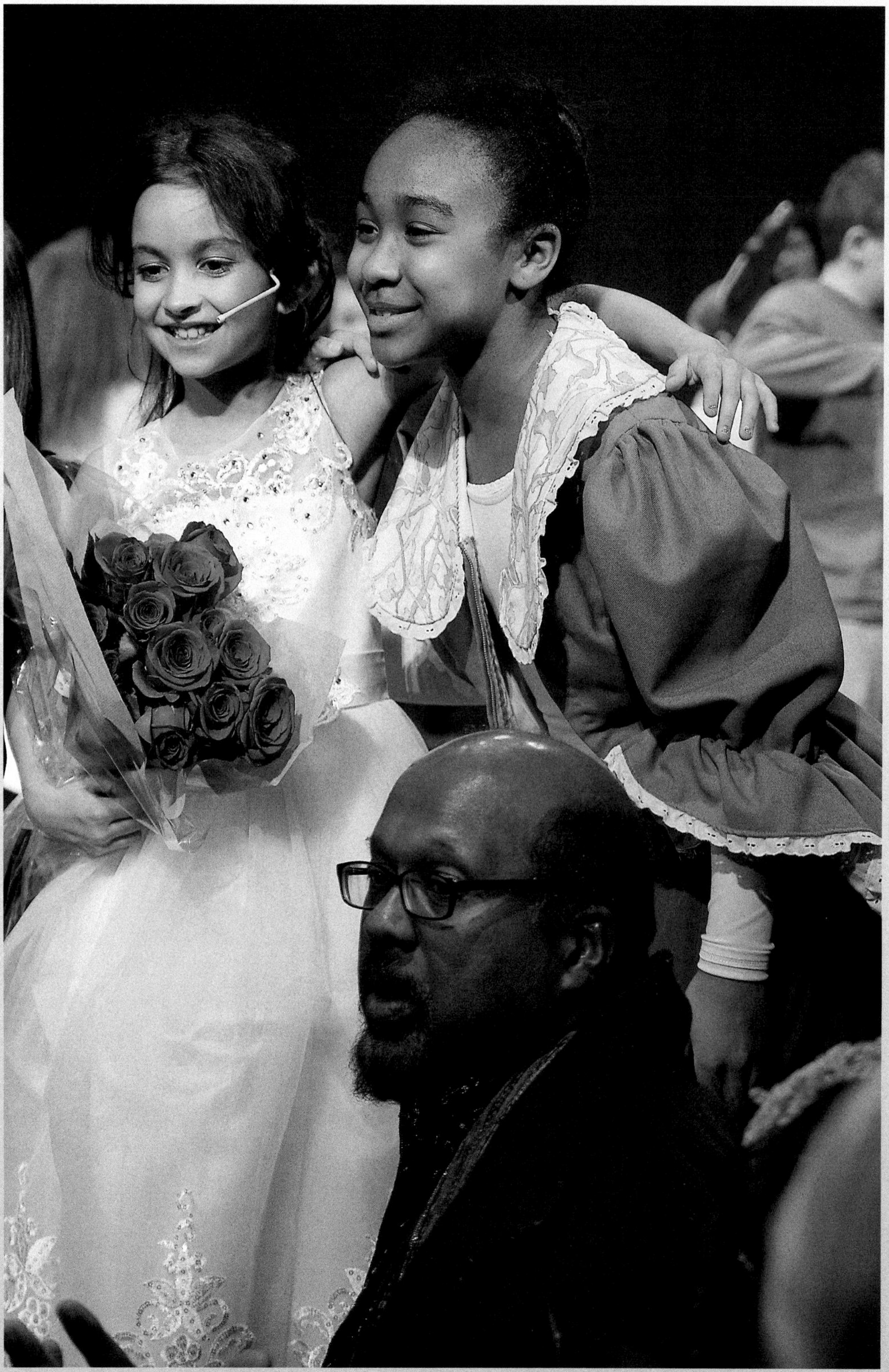

Belle, Mrs Potts (Asyah), and a proud Nana

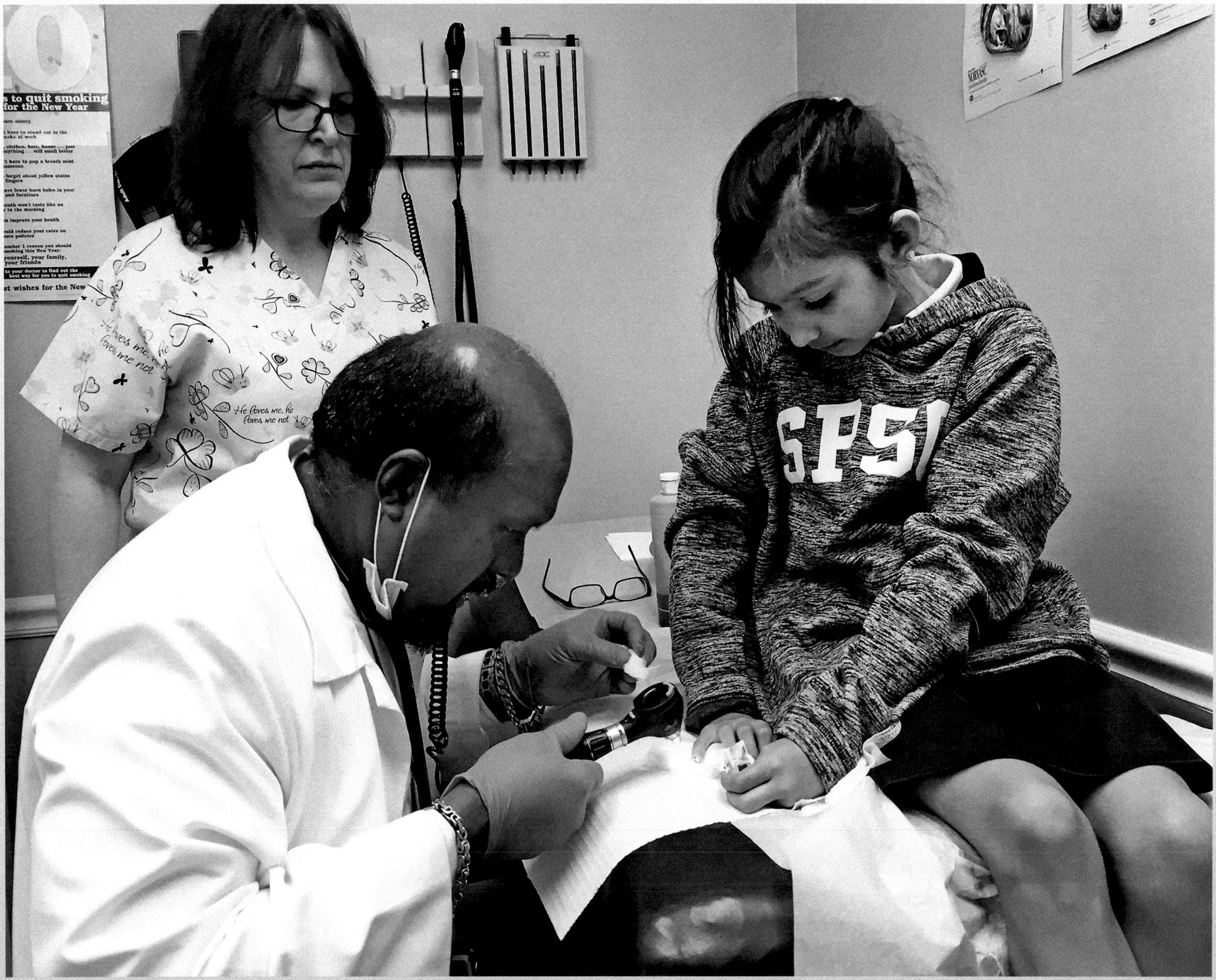


Dr. Nana in his surgery

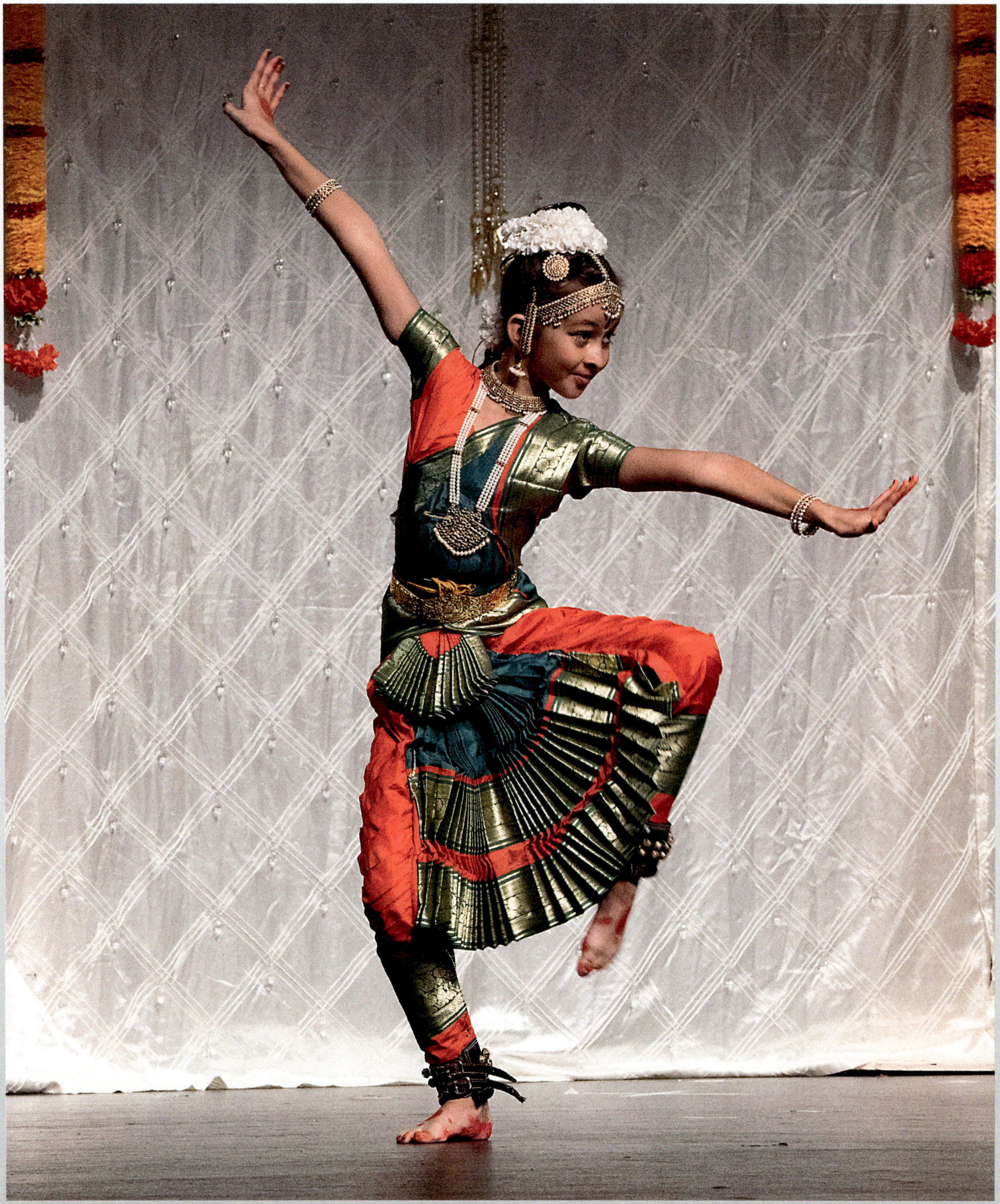

2019 Diwali Solo at ten



2019/10/26, 7:07:03 pm

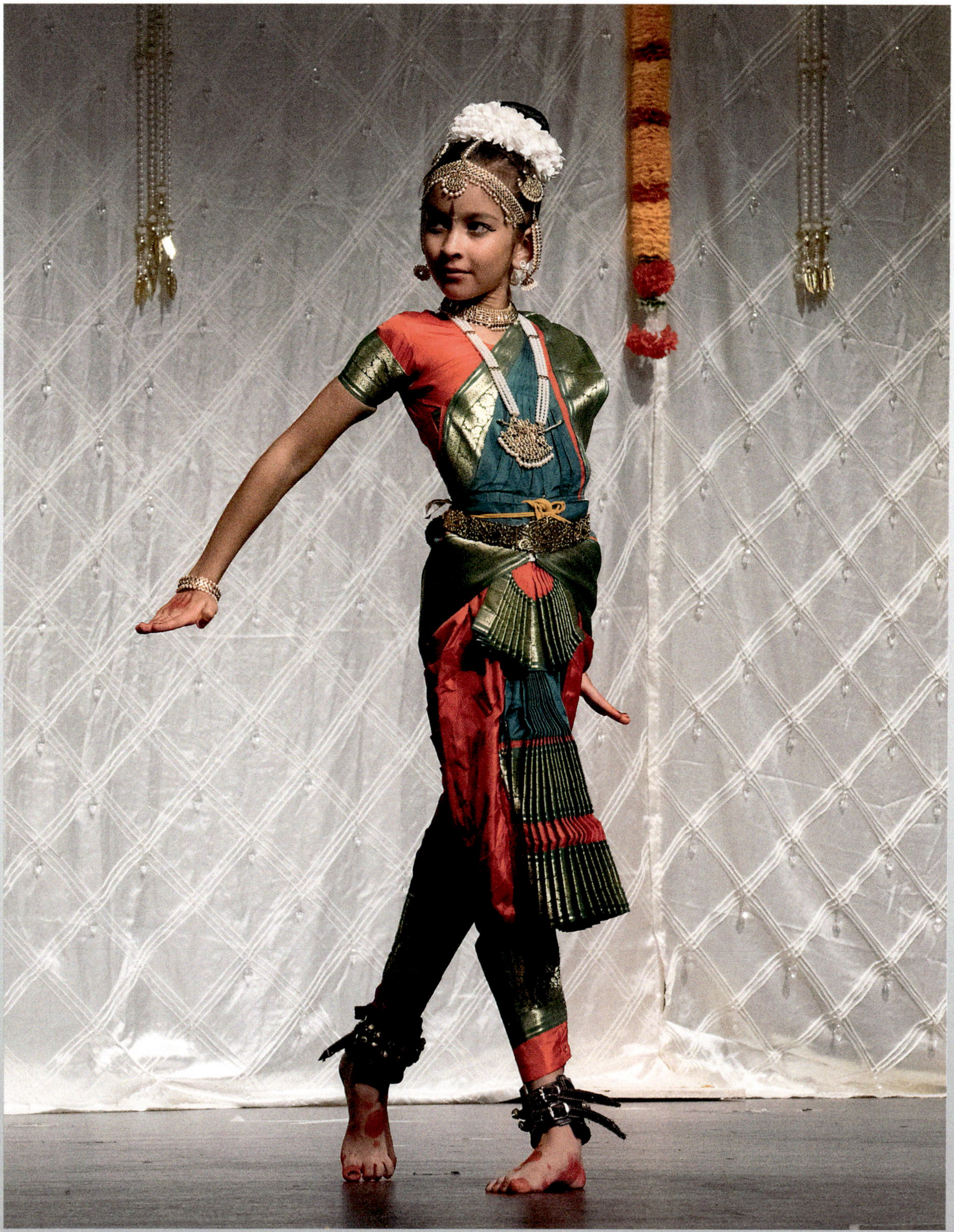

2019/10/26, 7:08:42 pm

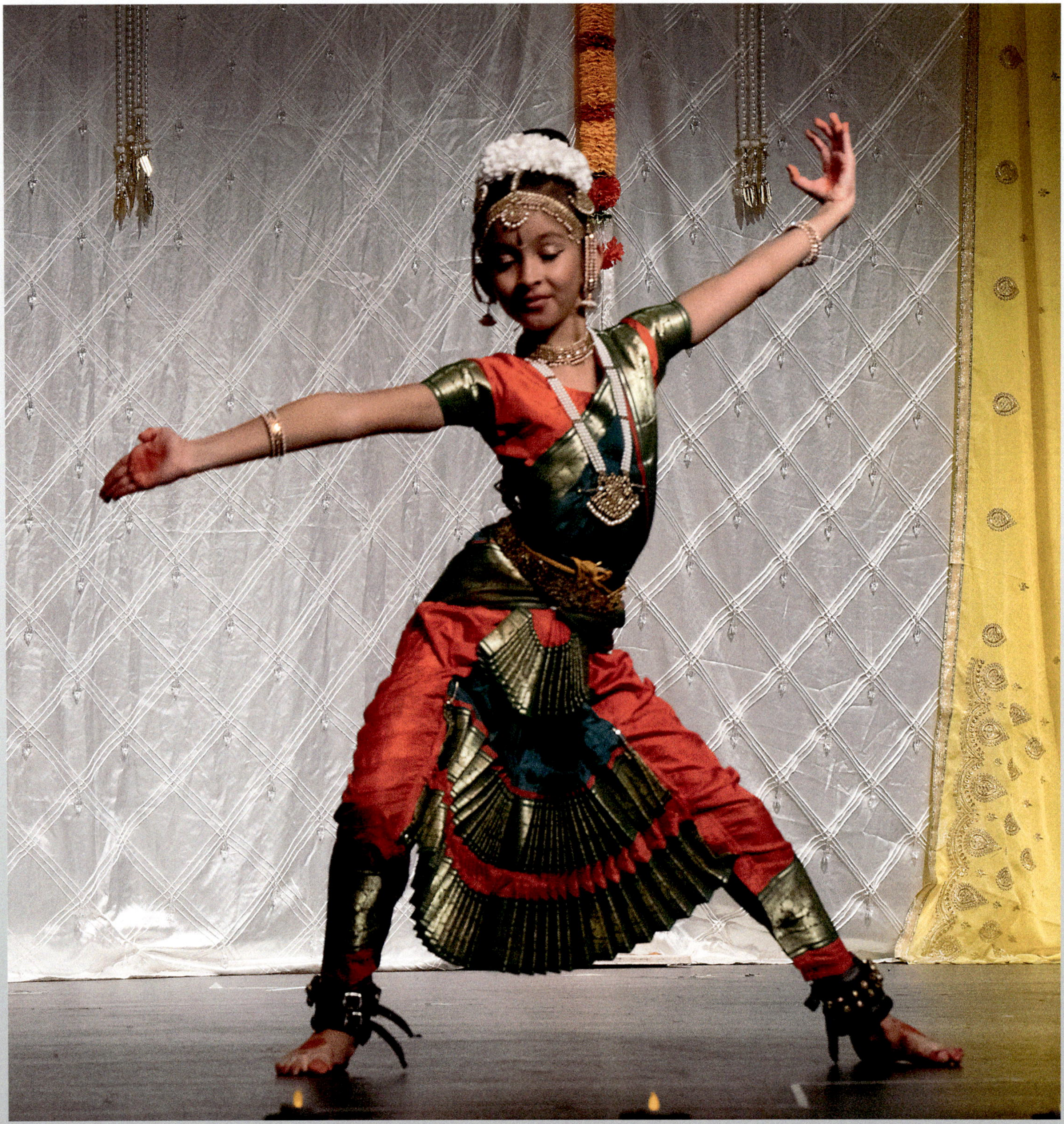

2019/10/26, 7:09:34 pm

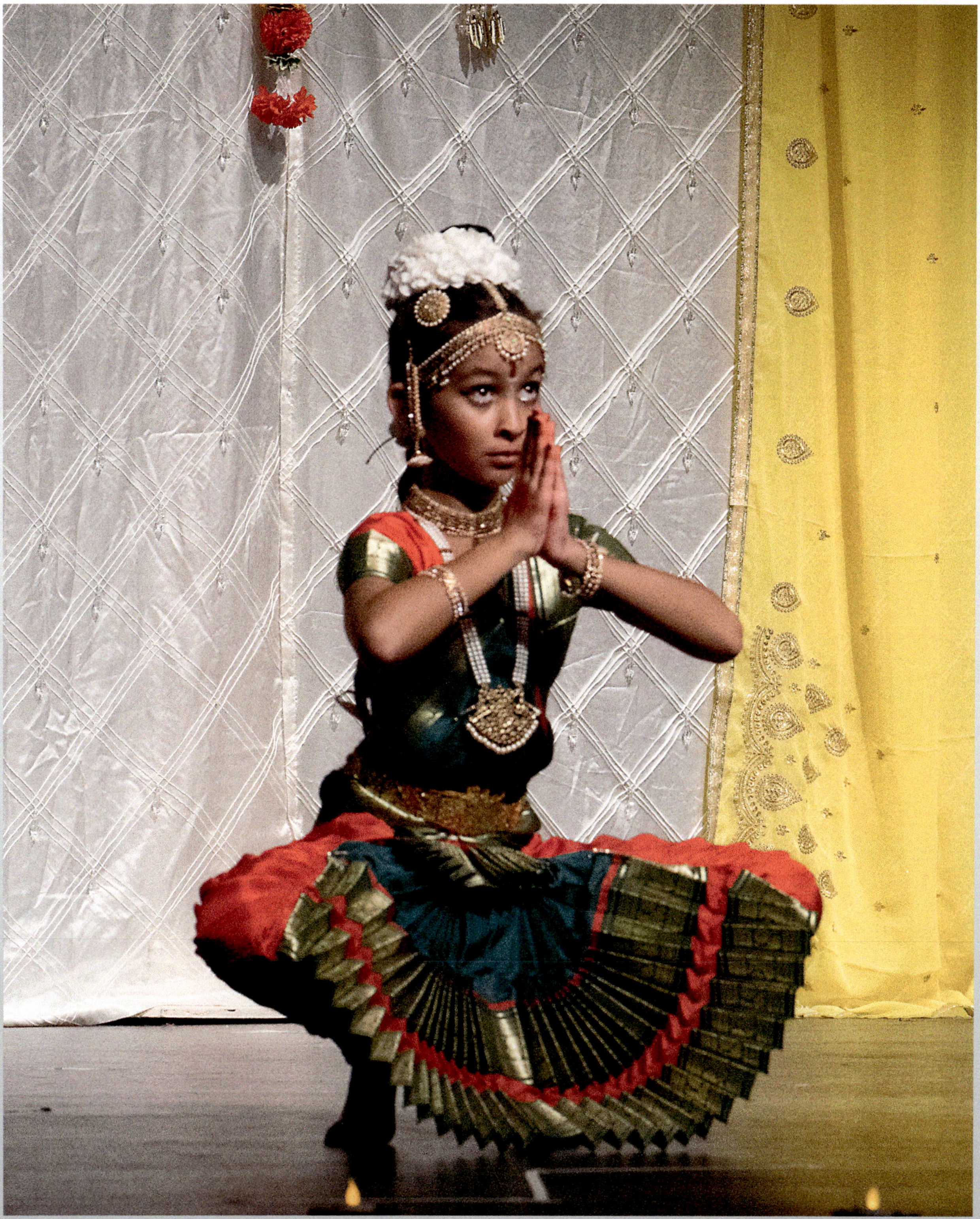

2019/10/26, 7:10:14 pm

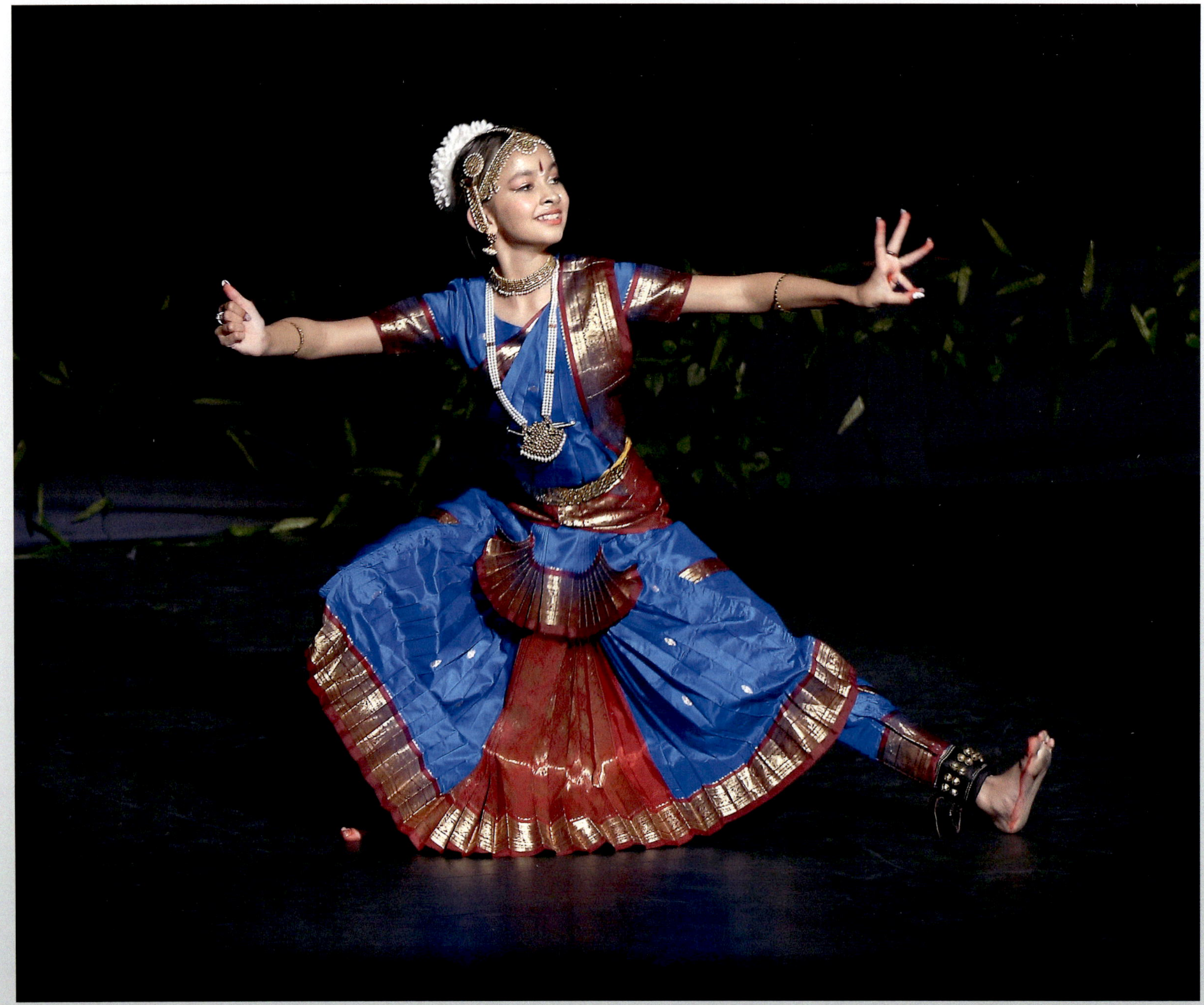

Guest solo performance in The Jungle Book production at age 12

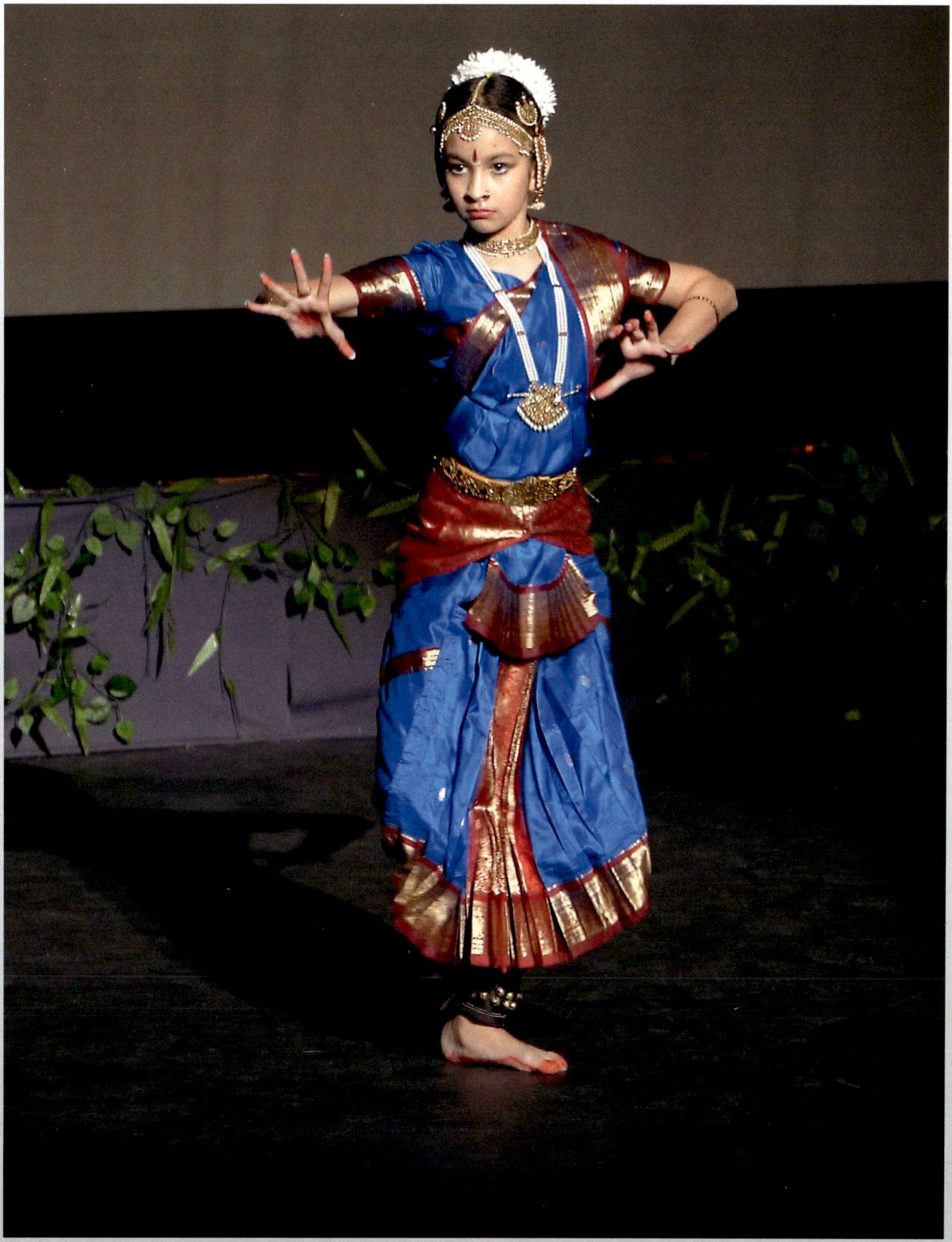

The Fearsome Tiger

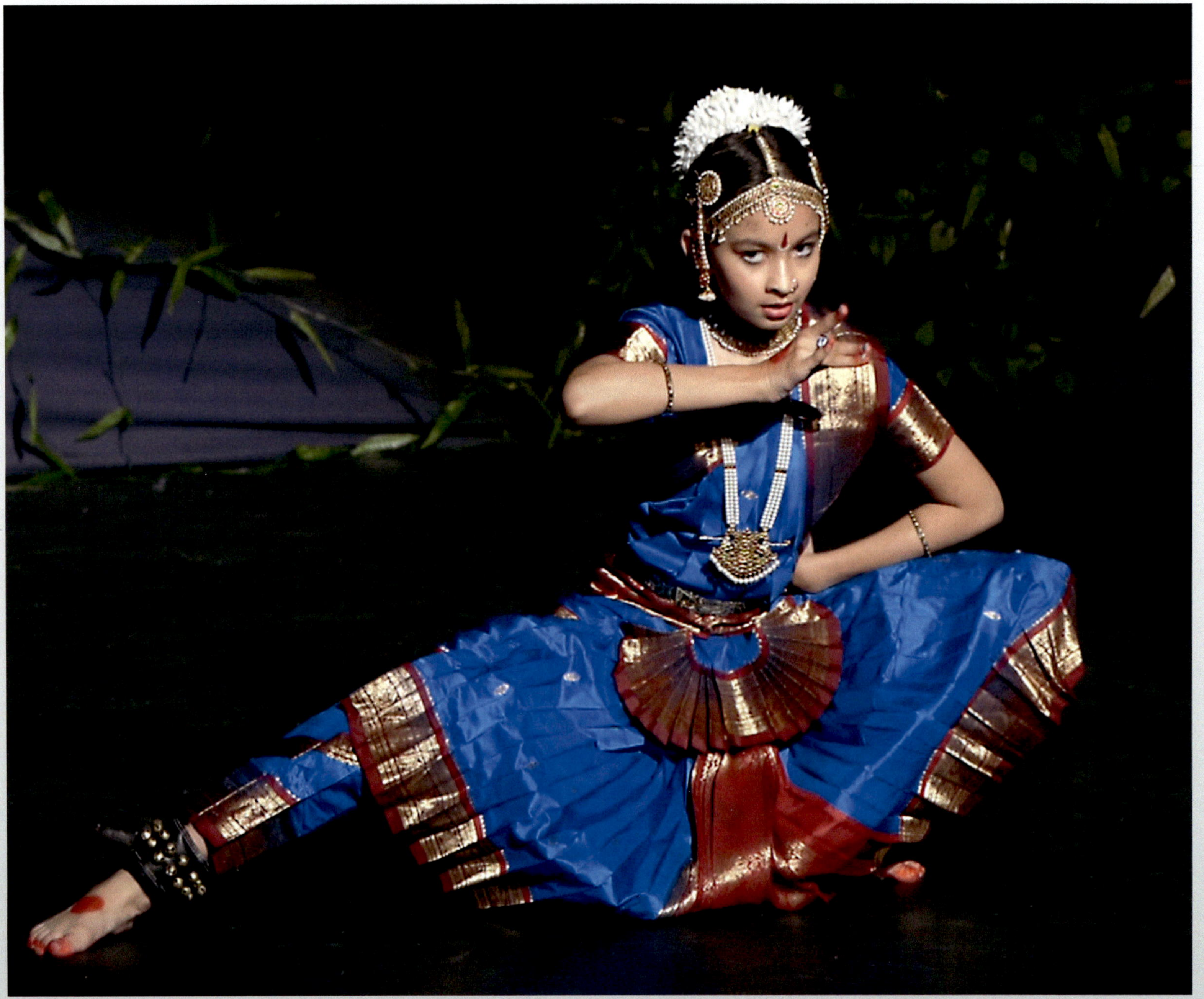

The Prowling Wolf

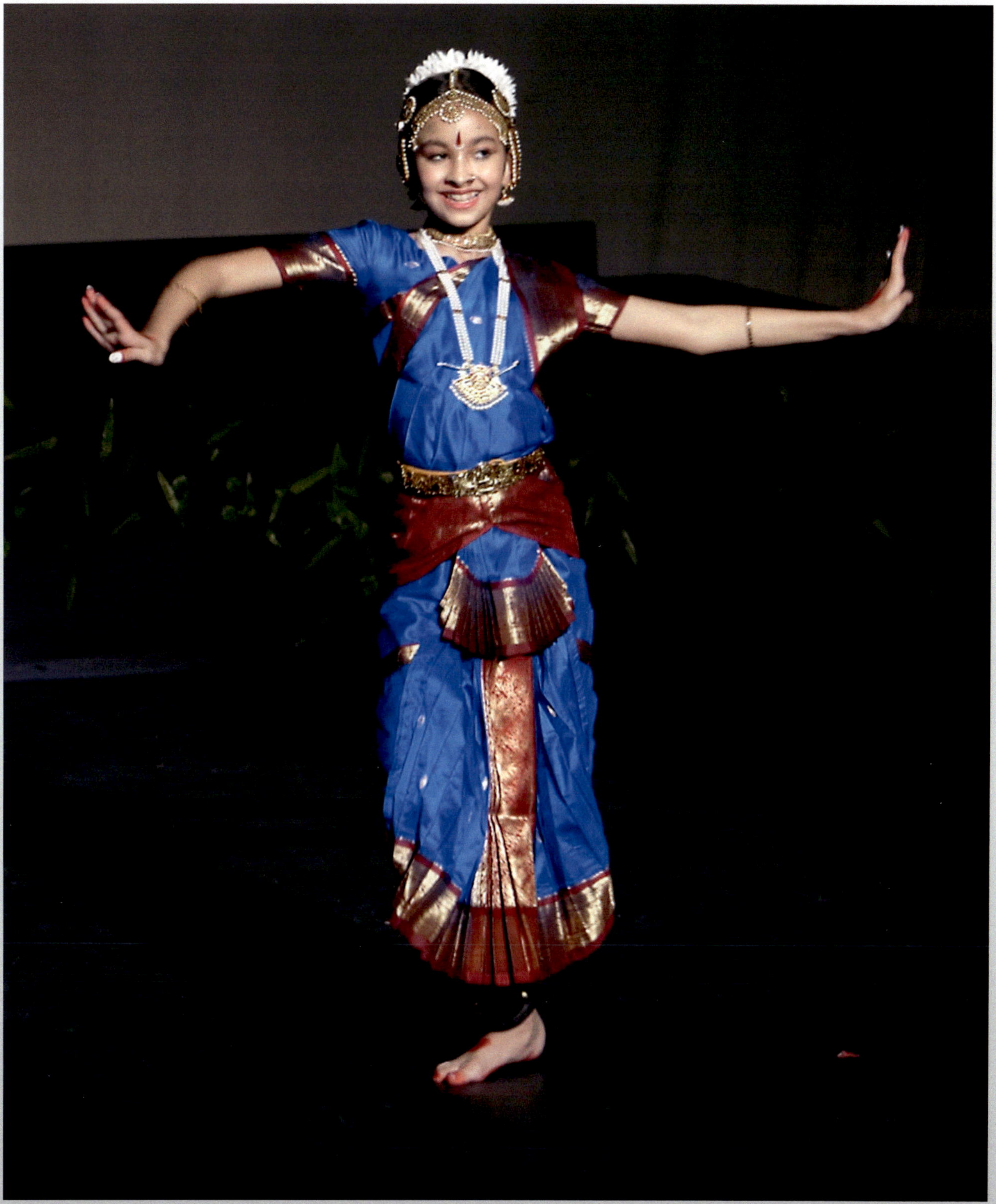

The Beguiling Snake

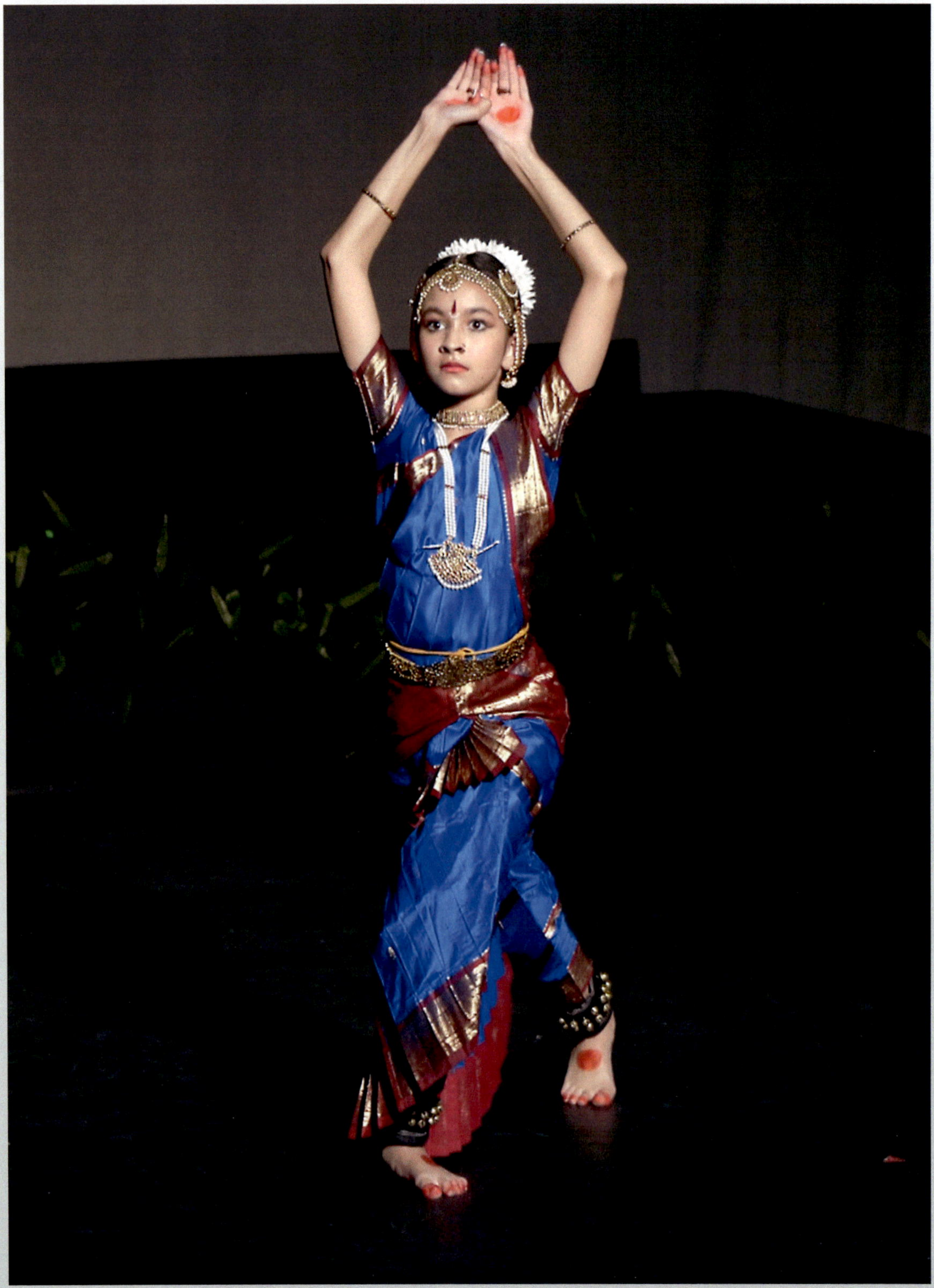

The Threatening Snake

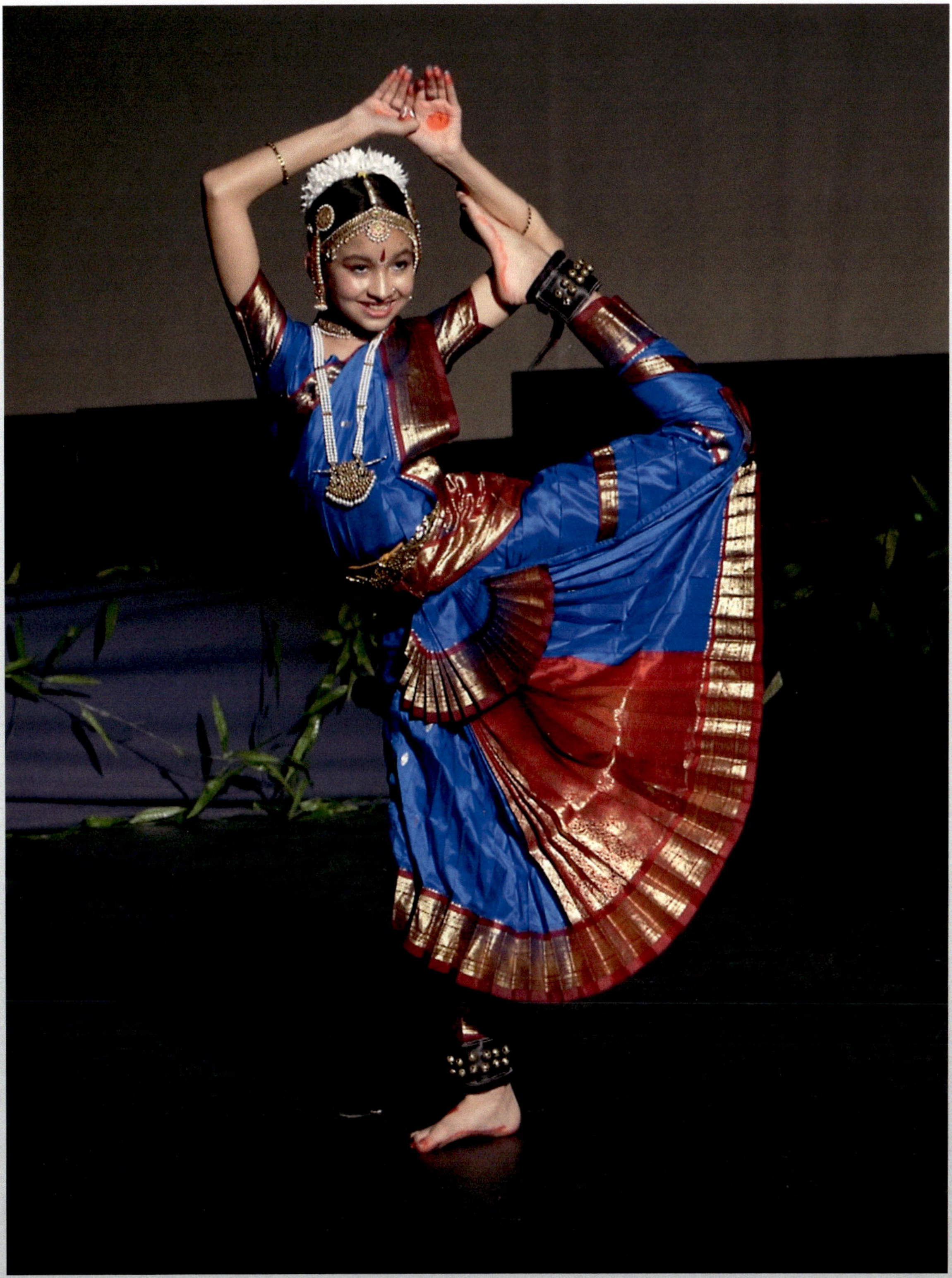

Final pose

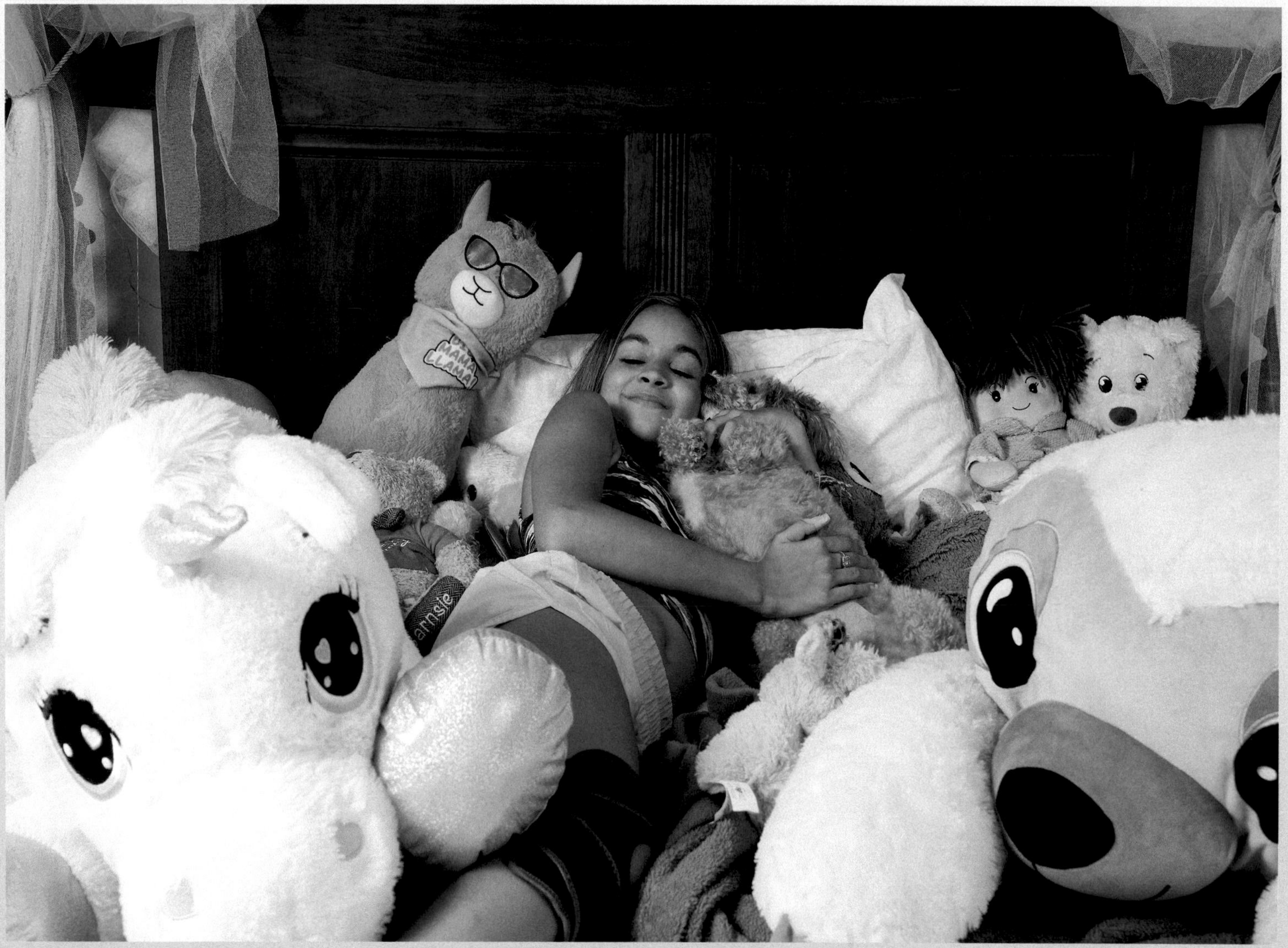

A live one among the toys

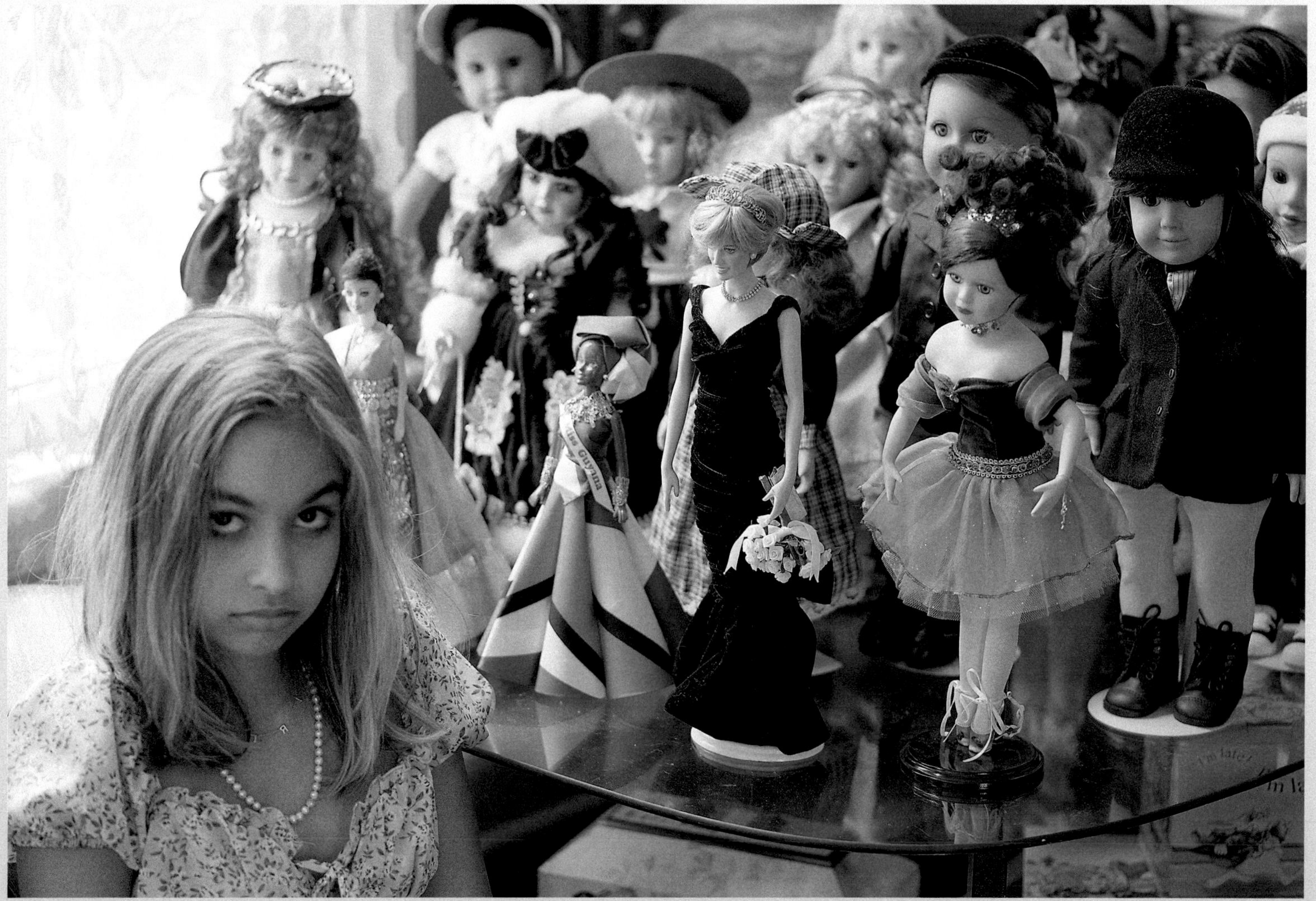

Dolls

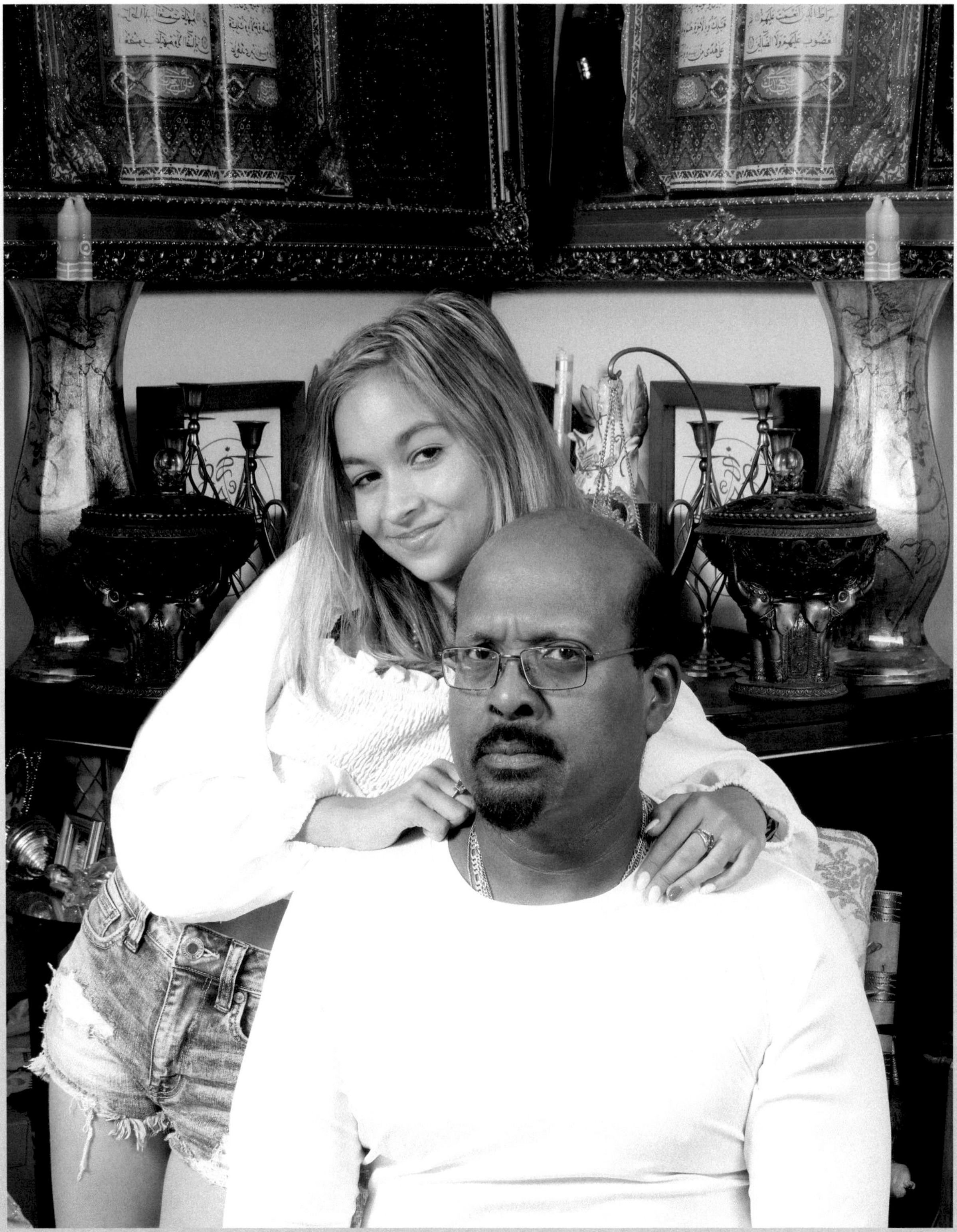

Don't mess with Nana!

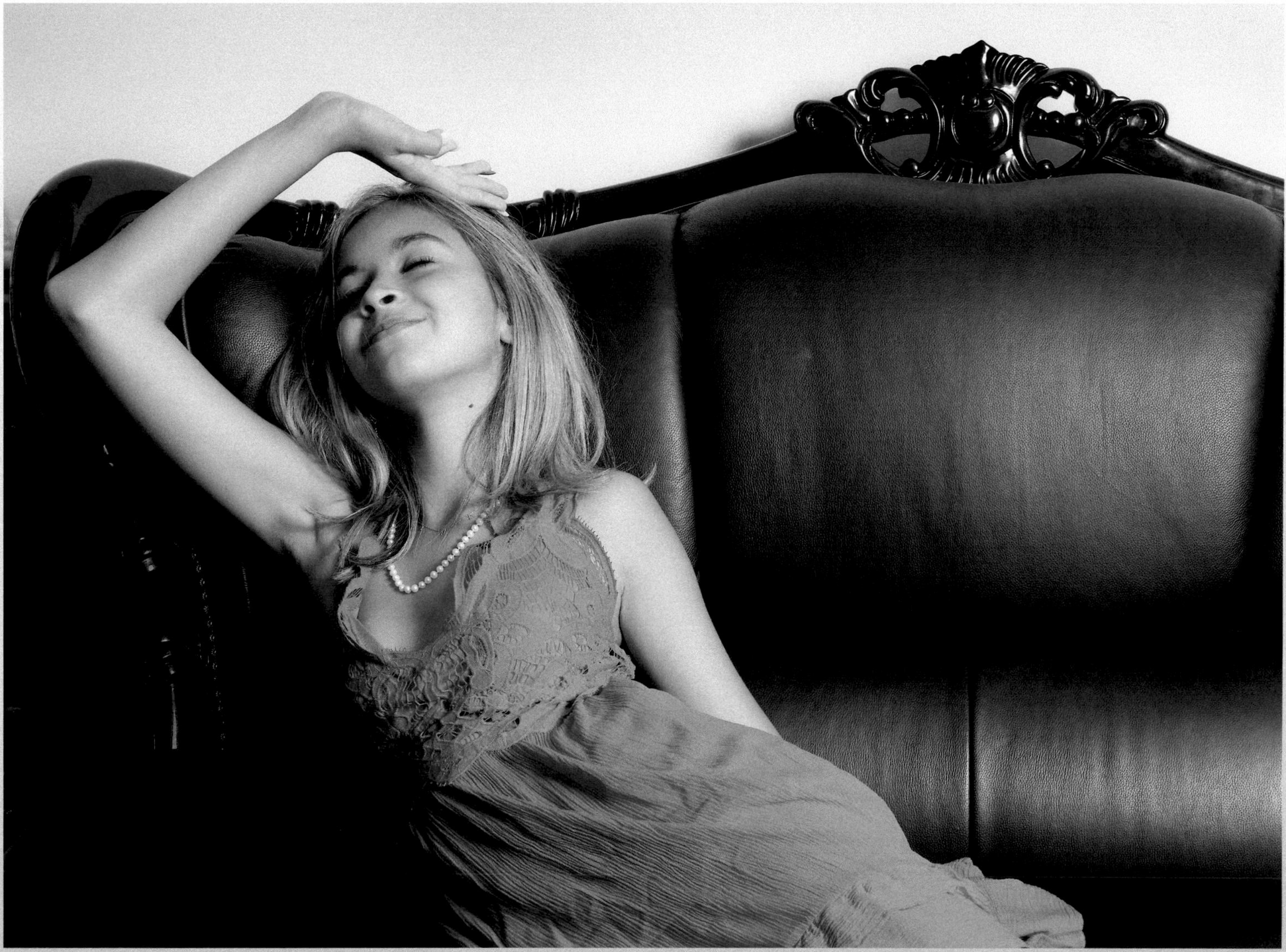

The swoon

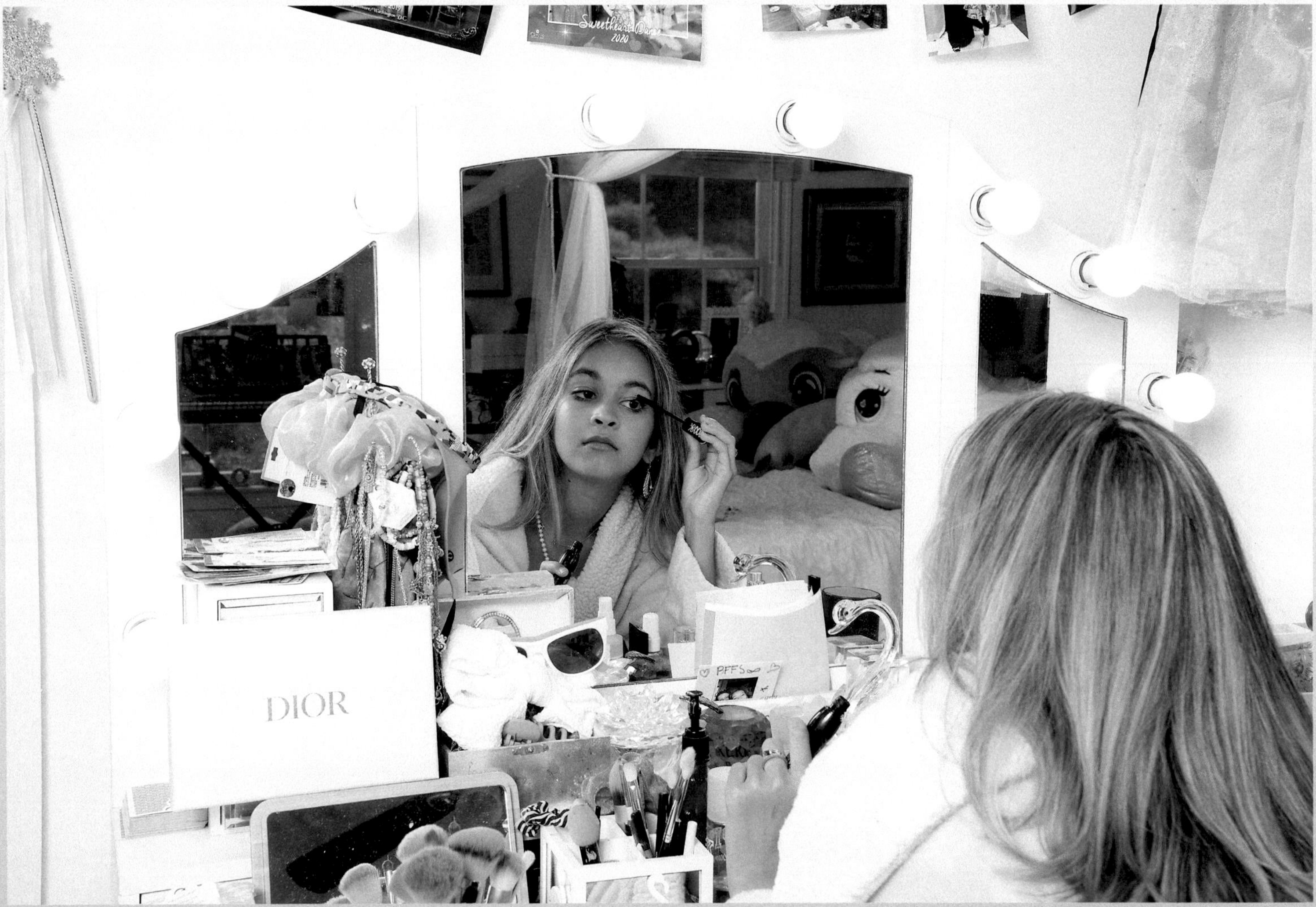




2022/07/29, 1:58:08 pm

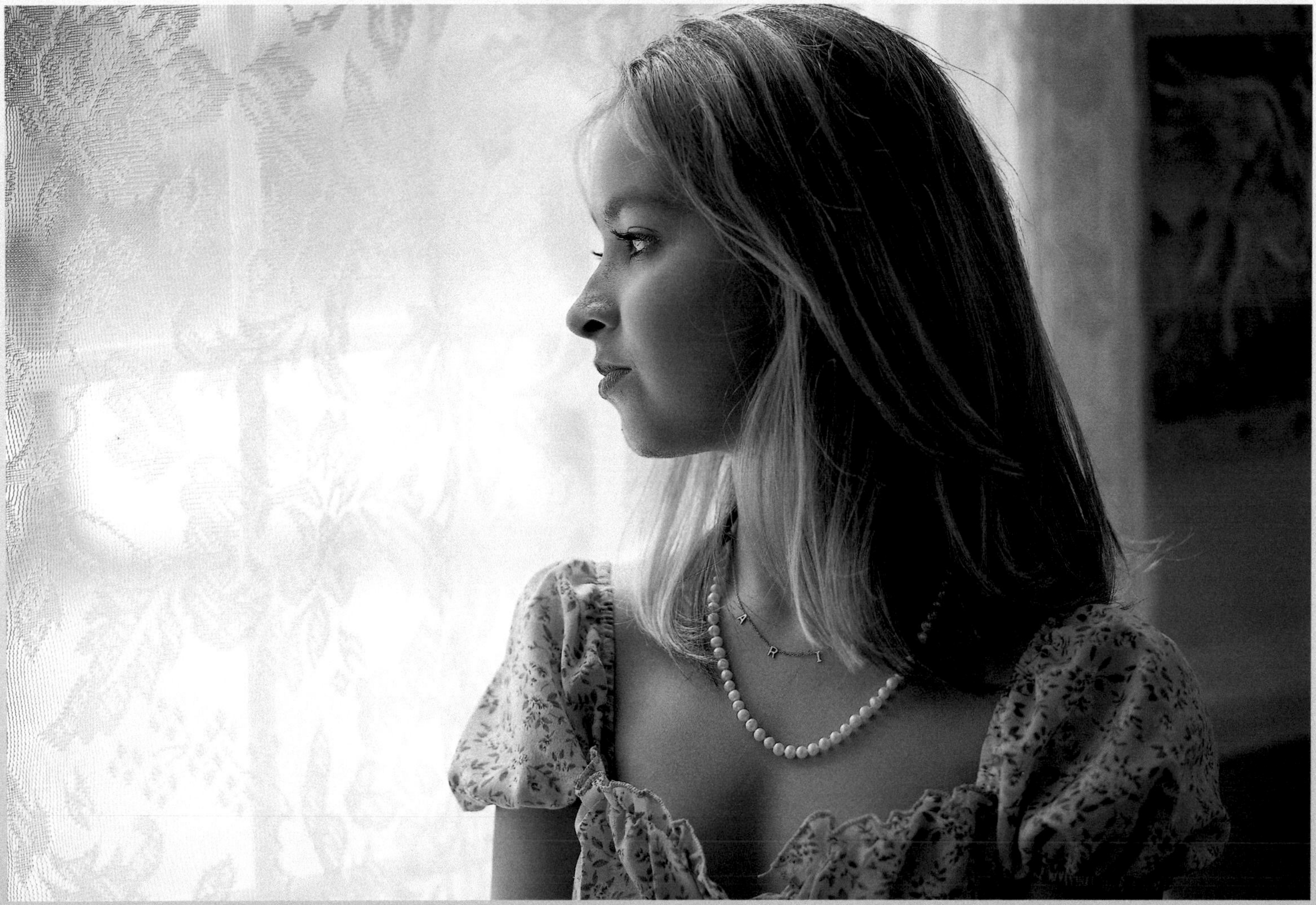

Looking back, shortly before her 13th birthday

# Acknowledgments

Above all, I would like to thank Nan Odie (Mama) for making these photoshoots possible. Besides making time in her schedule, she endured with patient grace my rearranging her furniture and relocating pictures on her wall. She was also instrumental in providing the vital wardrobe function. My wife Gail, as related in the Preface, was crucial in overcoming Aryani's initial reluctance to participate as a model as well as in helping with wardrobe and scheduling. Without their help, this book would not have happened.

I also have to acknowledge my debt to the inspiring photographs of Charles Dodgson, who wrote the Alice in Wonderland series under the pen name of Lewis Carroll in the mid-nineteenth century. Dodgson was an amateur but quite serious photographer, making some three thousand negatives over a twenty-four year period and meticulously documenting the circumstances of each.

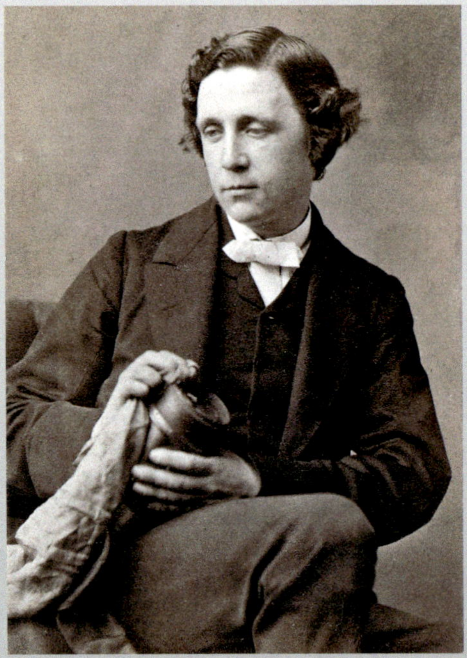

Lewis Carroll as photographed by Oscar Gustave Rejlander in 1863

Public Domain Image, https://commons.wikimedia.org/wiki/File:Lewis_Carroll_1863.jpg

Dodgson began photographing in 1856 after securing employment as a lecturer in mathematics at Christ Church, Oxford College. Within a year he began photographing the three young daughters, especially Alice, of Henry Liddell, the new dean of Christ Church. His first photographs of her were at age five. My favorite is this one from the summer of 1860 when she was eight years old.

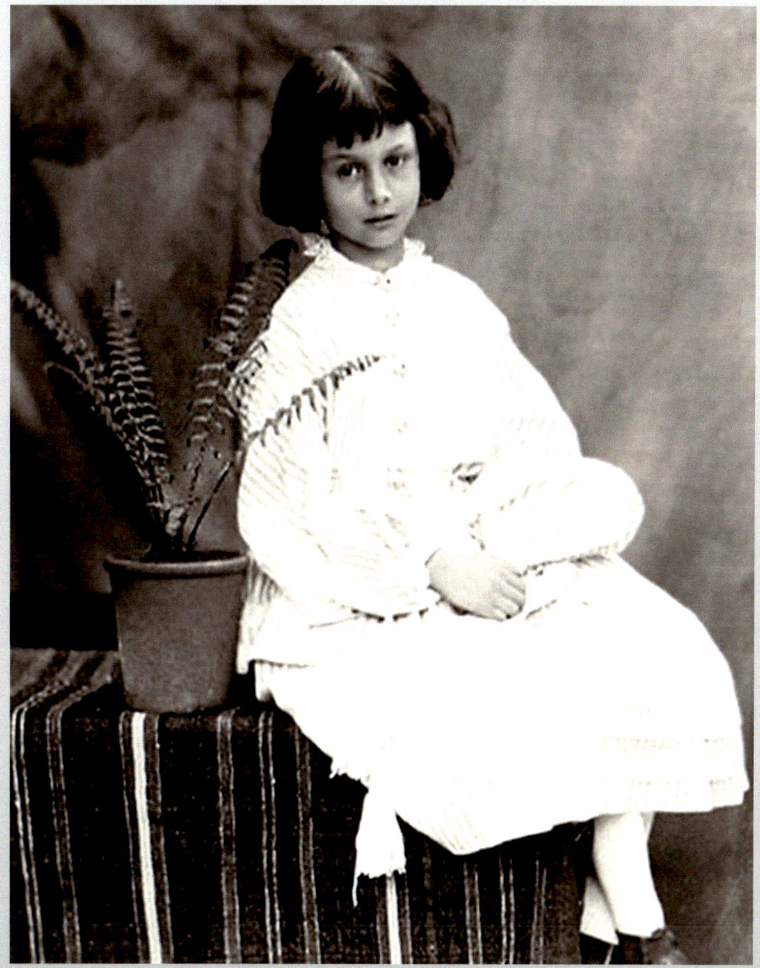

Lewis Carroll's photograph of Alice Liddell and Fern in July 1860

Public Domain Image, https://commons.wikimedia.org/w/index.php?curid=275464

The story goes that in the summer of 1862 Dodgson and his friend Rev. Robinson Duckworth rowed the three Liddell sisters up the Isis river for a picnic, and Dodgson entertained the girls with a fantastical story that he reputedly made up as they went along. His principal character was named Alice and the real Alice implored him to write it down. By the end of November of 1864 he had presented Alice with a hand-written manuscript as a gift. Subsequent revisions resulted in its being published in 1865 as Alice's Adventures in Wonderland. Since that time it has never been out of print.

Dodgson made many images of Alice, her sisters, as well as other children and adults, but for me the photograph shown on the previous page has no peer. There is something enigmatic about Alice's pensive expression. There is also a self-confidence and assertive quality about her presence that is quite exceptional for an eight-year-old. Aryani is blessed with these same character traits in addition to a playful sense of humor that imparts a radiant joyfulness to her personality. I can only hope that this book does justice to the richness of her spirit.

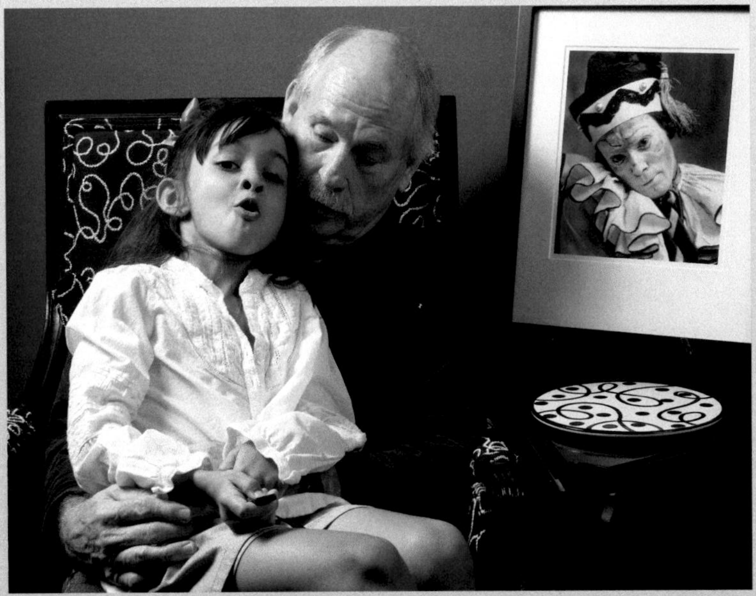

2016/10/20, 12:18:01 pm

Aryani and Martin horsing around during a photoshoot break. Note the camera remote trigger in her right hand; she took this picture. Modeling is hard work but she made each session fun with her playful antics.

When the day becomes the night
and the sky becomes the sea,
when the clock strikes heavy
and there's no time for tea;
and in our darkest hour,
before my final rhyme,
she will come back home to Wonderland
and turn back the hands of time.

—Alice Through the Looking Glass*

* This quote seems like it might have come from the hand of Lewis Carroll, inasmuch as the sentiment is sympathetic with the epigraph on page 6, albeit a bit more somber in tone. Alas, it does not. It actually is from the first (2015) trailer of Tim Burton's movie, Alice Through the Looking Glass, released in 2016. It is included here to evoke the fleeting nature of life and time as poignantly reflected in the pages of this book. I can easily imagine Aryani's emotions as she looks back at this book when she is my current age of 78.

The Chelsea Press